Electronic Frequencies and Mind Control

What Science, Psychology and Academia *Can't* Tell the Public

By

Endall Beall

First Edition

Copyright © 2021 Endall Beall

All Rights Reserved

ISBN- 9798718541717

Imprint: Independently published

DEDICATION

This book is dedicated to anyone who can envision a brighter future for all humanity and a world without tyranny in any form.

Table of Contents

ACKNOWLEDGEMENTS

I want to thank the patrons at our Patreon website for their input on some of the chapter previews and I want to offer my heartfelt thanks for those who helped edit this book. Everyone's contributions are valuable beyond measure. To everyone who contributed I offer my deepest gratitude.

FOREWORD

The book you have in your hand is filled with challenging ideas, most of which you have probably not encountered before or even contemplated. You are about to embark upon a journey into perceptual advancement and very likely learn more about humanity and yourself than you ever considered before or even gave thought to – perhaps more than you even wanted to know.

As you read this book you will find much you agree with wholeheartedly when you apply it to other people, but the challenge is whether you are a big enough individual to apply the same principles to yourself and learn from the experience by performing an honest self-analysis and realize that you are not magically exempt from the same behaviors you criticize in others to one degree or another. No one has a problem casting aspersions or criticism on others, but few indeed are big enough to *own* their own behaviors as quickly as they are willing to blame and castigate others for the same shortcomings. It is this ownership that this book aims to educate the public with. If you are not a strong enough individual to take a good hard look in the mirror at how you are being emotionally manipulated just like everyone else on this planet, then don't read this book, you won't learn anything from it. Your personal denial will keep you enslaved to the type of emotional psychological manipulation that this book seeks to expose, and give the reader pause to consider and grow beyond such manipulation of their own psyche by forces whose only goal is to control you and your culture.

There is information in this book that is going to disrupt your worldview. The initial emotional reactions you may feel once you digest the information in this book are liable to make you very uncomfortable, both emotionally and psychologically. This will not be an easy read for anyone who believes that all is right with the world. The information in this book, for many readers, is going to turn their world on its head and many will find what is revealed in these pages very troubling and hard to accept. Whether one accepts the truths offered in this book or not, it will not alter the reality that the information in these pages presents. The reader can either face the unpleasant information presented, or they can deny it. Denying it won't alter the facts, it only means that one is unwilling to accept the ugly truth presented in these pages.

INTRODUCTION

Human beings are herd animals. Reading these words probably sparked an immediate emotional reaction in you, most likely coupled with a desire to jump to your own defense by claiming that *you* are *not* a herd animal, but an *individual*! There is nary a human being on this planet that will not feel the same reaction you do when reading the opening sentence and the emotional bravado that arises in your claim to be an individual as a counter-argument. This is but one example of how we are each manipulated by emotions and self-image. Those who are in the business of controlling the masses of the human herds are fully aware of how to psychologically manipulate the public through emotional reactions, and it is the purpose of this book to illustrate how all of us have been subjected to this type of emotional psychological manipulation throughout our lives. Examples will be given from a real-world perspective based on observable behaviors that will be undeniable when viewed from a genuinely logical (unemotional) and objective standpoint.

To prove that we are herd animals we only need to look as far as how we identify ourselves. Each and every one of us uses one type of herd categorization or another to define ourselves. These herd identifiers are found in our religious beliefs, our political beliefs, our union associations (if one belongs to a union), our nationality and our traditions and the list goes on. We don't hear people say I believe in Christianity or Islam; they say I *am* a Christian or a Muslim. They don't believe in the Republican or Democrat party, they say I *am* a Republican or I *am* a Democrat. These few examples should be enough to illustrate my point. Regardless of your claim of individuality, that individuality is predicated on your being a part of some class or herd of other human beings who think and believe as you do. If you are a lone wolf type and feel that you are somehow exempt from this herd-oriented self-identification, if you claim to be a Frenchman, or a Briton, an American or an Indian, the national herd identity still serves to shape part of your individual identity and personality.

Along with the varied and multiple herd identities that coalesce to create your individual identity comes the emotional necessity to defend the herd beliefs that you embrace to define yourself, for to challenge the belief challenges your own individuality. This is why everyone becomes emotionally defensive when their most cherished beliefs are challenged by another. There is no rationale involved when one is emotionally defending a belief, for to defend the belief amounts to the individual defending themselves from a perceptual attack by the challenger. All these factors that we embrace as our multiple beliefs, are what is referred to as cultural identity. Within any national culture there are multitudes of subcultures such as unions, religions, political affiliations, sports team associations and fans, and the list goes on and on. Every individual is little more than a conglomeration of beliefs used to shape their personal identity.

Although the degree of defensiveness to specific issues may vary from person to person, each of us has certain emotional soft spots that, once triggered by an outside challenger, create an emotional reaction, sometimes very intense, whereby we must jump to defend our most cherished beliefs, and thus defend ourselves because we *become* our beliefs. It is through deliberate psychological manipulation delivered via many varied avenues of our lives that those who know how to, and demand to control the human herds, can steer entire populations through emotional incitement to do their bidding. All the controlling party has to do is find a group of individuals' emotional soft spot and they can induce a nation to go to war or turn on their own countrymen.

In my book *The Psychology of Becoming Human: Transcending the Psychology of the Gods*, I capably illustrated how the field of psychology has been used as a weapon against humanity since its inception as a soft science. This type of psychological manipulation would have little to no power without the ability to incite emotions in any given target audience. It is through psychological emotional manipulation and control that the so-called global elite, the 1%, control the other 99% of humanity. This has been done throughout human history.

The majority of people on this planet do not function from the standpoint of reason and logic, they are governed by their emotions. When anyone learns how to 'push your buttons' emotionally, then they gain control over your consciousness. Many readers have found this to be true in their personal relationships, and we have all become experts at emotional manipulation ourselves. Emotions are the hidden language of control. The words and methods we all use to gain this emotional power over others varies from person to person, but we all learn at an early age how to use emotions to get what we want from others. At first you may choose to deny this assertion, but every human being on the planet is guilty of using such emotional manipulation against others in their life. This book is designed to provide a layman's analysis of how this all works and will suggest how, before humanity can advance into a more emotionally stable species, we must reassess how we function and move beyond what misguided psychologists consider the human norm where our emotions are concerned.

1. We Learn Early

While we are still in the crib, each of us soon learns how to get what we want from our parents or guardians. We discover very quickly that if we want to be picked up and coddled, or if we want to be fed or have our diapers changed, that all we need to do is cry. It takes an infant a very short window of time to learn this tactic of manipulation. People respond to crying babies. From this starting point of using the emotion of displeasure from discomfort, or merely wanting to be picked up and held, we advance through varying stages developing our skills of emotional manipulation.

The next level of a child emotionally manipulating their parents occurs when they learn the word *no*. By learning the word no the child learns to exert some of its own control, or believes it does, by its first challenge to authority (which is eventually programmed out of us in later life, unfortunately). Once a child learns the word 'no', then the developmental battle of wills starts between parent and child until the rebelliousness is subdued and the child is given its first lessons in authoritarianism. Parents who fail to turn this rebellion into more responsible and positive behaviors usually wind up with a child they can't control, which leads to greater problems in later life with a child who grows up with no concept of responsibility and an extreme sense of entitlement. Welcome to the Millennial generation and the subsequent generations exerting their entitlement mentality on the world political stage.

I am not a child psychologist, but what I have observed personally when I see children raised without a certain amount of discipline (and yes, I sanction spanking when it is warranted), is that they more often turn into emotionally predatory adults than not. Without that instilled sense of discipline and personal responsibility, our culture has bred generations of self-entitled radical victims. My observation is that many of these entitled radical victims come from middle class homes whose parents were too light-handed in the discipline department in teaching their kids personal responsibility. There are many reasons for this which I will endeavor to cover in the pages of this book, revealing a tyranny that will shock the conscious of the reader.

On the flip side of this entitlement mentality, we have those who come from split families where a mother may work two or three jobs and who just doesn't have the time to educate their children in responsible behavior. Some of this reaches into the more impoverished classes in our society and also creates its own form of victim mentality based on race or cultural class distinctions. The undisciplined child will mature into a basically undisciplined adult who possesses an extreme sense of self-entitlement and cares not about the feelings of others nor the generally accepted rules of cultural civility.

Childhood abuse often, but not always, creates multigenerational abusers. Some are fortunate enough to break free of this and choose to not become abusers themselves, but in many cases, they turn into the parents who swing too far in the other direction and choose to not discipline their children at all, once again creating the 'wild child' who runs roughshod over their parents and moves into the world becoming an entitlement-oriented emotional abuser themselves. We see this on massive display in the arena of radical Social Justice Warriors (SJWs) who populate our college campuses today.

In all fairness, all of these SJW emotional abusers are not necessarily the fault of bad parenting. Much of the responsibility for this lies directly on the shoulders of Marxist ideologues who have risen to high position in our colleges and universities and who are experts at indoctrinating young people into becoming victim-oriented political activists. This is particularly true in the so-called Humanities courses. The Marxist-controlled university system is populated with Marxist Communist professors and administrators. I will discuss this more later.

While we have armies of child psychologists seeking to get into the 'mind' of the child, I have not seen any theories in my reading on the subject (which is far from extensive) where these psychologists are looking at emotions as a driving force in the minds of children. They are working from an inverted picture in my estimation, by believing it is the mind that manages the emotions, when in fact I believe it to be exactly the opposite. Human beings react emotionally first, before virtually any thinking process ever engages. As such, we are all easy to manipulate by inflaming our emotions through fear and perceptions of being victimized by others.

"Give me a child until he is 7 and I will show you the man." Although this particular quote has been erroneously attributed to the creator of the Jesuit Order, Ignatius Loyola, it actually finds its origin with the Greek philosopher Aristotle. I introduce this point to illustrate that the child's formative years up to the age of 7 are what establishes the framework of their personal 'programming' that follows them through their lives. Aristotle was born in 384 BC, so this concept of shaping the minds of children is at minimum 2,350 years old.

From 600-300 BC the Greek philosophers started investigating the human mind through speculations that eventually led to the creation of the field of Psychology in the late 19th to early 20th centuries. These philosophers were the first people we are aware of to speculate that mental illnesses were more psychological in nature than they were attributable to supernatural forces such as demon possessions – the belief in which has followed humanity to this day in certain religions and superstitious belief systems.

The shaping of young minds has always been a focus of those who desired to set the direction of their cultures and maintain their cultural traditions, religions and social organization in both government and the household. Since the creation of the public-school systems in the 20th century, Marxist ideologues have worked ceaselessly to slowly percolate their leftist ideologies into American classrooms and worldwide. They have hidden behind such innocuous words as Progressivism to trick the public into believing they represent progress, but their only objective in this progress is the furtherance of Marxist ideology and the destruction of cultures around the world by destroying them from within. The major perpetrators of this slow, erosive endeavor started with a group of upper middle-class malcontents who fed on the Marxist ideology and formed a secret society in Great Britain in 1884 called the British Fabian Society. While others from the school of Marx's ideas promoted more active and violent revolution, the Fabian Society felt that Marx's goals could be better achieved through gradual subversive means to slowly 're-educate' the world into the Marxist belief system leading to the target populations virtually begging to be part of a world government devised by these calculating visionaries who had dreams of ruling the world. This Marxist ideology in modern vernacular is, like Progressivism, Marxism hidden by another name – i.e. Globalism.

In order to achieve their gradualist agenda, the Fabian Society knew that it was going to have to gain control over the educational system in order to start brainwashing the public into Marxist ideologies. The Fabians knew that to perform their form of gradualist social engineering that they would not only have to control the teachers but must control the content of school textbooks. Enter Harold Rugg, a Progressive leftist ideologue who gained his notoriety by publishing left-leaning textbooks and fabricating the historical content of these books to undermine America's system of Constitutional government.

Rugg was challenged by the American Legion for his publishing of Progressive (Marxist) educational material working in tangent with the Fabian Society's agenda to socially engineer the world into accepting the Marxist Globalist agenda for world domination.

Coupled with Rugg's rise to power in the school textbook publishing agenda, the early psychologists, many of whom were directly associated with a sister organization of the Fabian Society called The Society for Psychical Research (SPR) which was created in 1882, were experimenting wholesale with every psychological means available to sway the thoughts of the American herds, using everything from advertising commercial products to eventually peddling a layman's version of psychology to hoodwink people into trusting the presumed healing abilities of Psychology.

In 1895, the first theory of Crowd Psychology was introduced by Gustave Le Bon in his book, *The Crowd: A Study of the Popular Mind*. Le Bon detested socialism and saw it as a pernicious replacement of religion as a form of secular religion, and he stated as much in no uncertain terms in his book, *The Psychology of Socialism*, which was published in 1898. Despite the fact that Le Bon personally hated Socialism, it did not prevent the Fabian Society and the SPR from latching on to his work in *The Crowd*, coupled with behavioral studies by Ivan Pavlov and his dogs in the 1890s, to start experimenting with shaping human herd perceptions through psychological means. Two members of the Society for Psychical Research moved into America and France, opening branches of the SPR in those countries. Each of these members, William James in America, and Pierre Janet in France, both became the 'Fathers of Psychology' in their respective countries.

The association between the advancements in the field of Psychology, the SPR and the Fabian Society is irrefutable by no shortage of evidence on the public record, although one does have to dig a little to find these connections as the Marxist Globalists would much prefer that these associations not be made to the public at large. In the midst of these connections just identified, we have a third factor that is most often overlooked, and that is with a group that peddles a form of intellectualist spiritualism called the Theosophical Society that was organized by the Russian medium, Madame Helena Blavatsky in 1875.

These three organizations, the Theosophical Society, the SPR and the Fabian Society have been incestuously interlinked since before 1882 when the SPR was officially organized, and their agenda has been the ultimate conquest of the world through psychological means to brainwash and control human thought through psychological manipulation and a form of mind control delivered at virtually every avenue of our lives. I realize how big a pill this is to swallow for the average uninformed person, but I provided more than enough substantive evidence of this continual undermining and control of human consciousness using Psychology as a weapon of war in my book, *The Psychology of Becoming Human: Evolving Beyond Psychological Conditioning*.

Although I established the abuse of psychology to serve as a social engineering control mechanism in my aforementioned book, particularly in Western societies, the same factors have been used in Communist regimes and are still being abused today. It's not that hard for people to admit the psychological control that exists in say, Communist China, or even the former Soviet Union, but Westerners are unwilling to admit that the same psychological weapons have been used against them for well over a century now by the same people who pushed those agendas in Communist countries in the past and present. If I try to tell someone they are mind-controlled, they will protest and kick and scream denying that such a thing is possible. They would swear up and down that such a thing is not remotely possible and that they are a free-thinking and independent individual. By the time you finish reading this book I should be able to prove to you that not only are such things possible, but that your mind is controlled by exterior forces far more sinister than you will probably be willing to face and accept, and that this psychological manipulation occurs because of how human beings use their emotions. This is going to be an unpleasant journey down a rabbit hole of reality that few are going to be willing to admit, but after producing the evidence in this book, I am certain that the only safe haven from accepting the truth presented herein will be simple denial. Denial of truth does not make it untrue; it only means we are unwilling to accept the truth when it is presented to us. As this book progresses, even the desire to deny the truth will be explained and you will understand why everyone chooses to deny rather than face the unpleasantness of hard, uncomfortable reality.

The primary purpose of this book is to lead the reader to a greater understanding of themselves as well as pointing a way out of the cognitive slavery in which we all live in our blissful ignorance. The reader is going to be confronted with concepts never delivered by science for the simple fact that science itself is operating in its own world of limited perceptions and an incorrect view of reality. This book is going to offer information that will cause the reader to put it down and contemplate deeply on the meaning of the information delivered. That is to be expected, for it is only when we take the information presented in this book and ponder what it means that the reader will be able to decide for themselves whether they want to remain controlled in the fashion that will be revealed, or whether they want to try and transcend this hidden tyranny and genuinely free their mind from this control.

Despite how fanciful such claims may initially appear, digesting the information in this book has the potential to shake the roots of your reality. My intent is not to shock the individual by raising wild claims, but to sow awareness so every reader is presented with an informed choice to continue living as they have been or choose to become something more than they ever imagined themselves to be. One can't find any kind of freedom until they understand how they have been enslaved. This book is going to explain how you have been enslaved by seduction and emotional control, for it is through our emotions that all psychological manipulation finds the platform to control the mind.

2. Perceptions of Mind Control

The best place to launch this discussion is with what humans perceive to be mind control. In its simplest terms, mind control is generally equated with brainwashing. Using Wikipedia's definition of *Brainwashing* we find:

> *"Brainwashing (also known as mind control, menticide, coercive persuasion, thought control, thought reform, and re-education) is the concept that the human mind can be altered or controlled by certain psychological techniques. Brainwashing is said to reduce its subject's ability to think critically or independently, to allow the introduction of new, unwanted thoughts and ideas into the subject's mind, as well as to change his or her attitudes, values, and beliefs.*

> *The concept of brainwashing was originally developed in the 1950s to explain how the Chinese government appeared to make people cooperate with them. Advocates of the concept also looked at Nazi Germany, at some criminal cases in the United States, and at the actions of human traffickers. It was later applied by Margaret*

Singer, Philip Zimbardo and some others in the anti-cult movement to explain conversions to some new religious movements and other groups. This resulted in scientific and legal debate with Eileen Barker, James Richardson, and other scholars, as well as legal experts, rejecting at least the popular understanding of brainwashing."

An interesting point to be noted from the people listed above is that Eileen Barker is a professor in sociology and an emeritus member of the London School of Economics (LSE). The LSE was created by the Fabian Society in 1895, so it should come as no surprise that she would be an advocate denouncing brainwashing as real. The LSE is a Marxist think tank, now associated with the University of London and was formed by some of the most radical Marxist members of the Fabian Society - Sidney Webb, Beatrice Webb, Graham Wallas, and George Bernard Shaw. For more information on the LSE look up London School of Economics on Wikipedia or through other sources to see their Marxist Socialist agenda. It should also be noted that Margaret Sanger was also a Fabian who created Planned Parenthood, which stands at the center of the political debate on abortion as a primary point of contention in the American political spectrum at this time.

A book written by William Sargant entitled, *Battle for the Mind: A Physiology of Conversion and Brain-Washing* was published in 1994 which explains in depth the process of trying to figure out the brainwashing techniques applied by the Chinese and

North Koreans after the Korean police action in the 1950s. This book is an excellent study in the efforts to discover whether brainwashing had lasting effects on a permanent basis or not for those interested in this study.

As the Wikipedia explanations advise us, the research and experimentation into mind control, at least on the governmental level, was launched in the 1950s, and one of the most well-known secret operations that has come to light in recent decades is the CIA's Project MK-Ultra. Through the MK-Ultra experiments it has been revealed that the CIA was using LSD and other drugs on their subjects seeking methods through which they could control their minds. Although this most blatant form of mind control is more widely known, recent documents that have come to light inform us that the MK-Ultra project also used mass mind-control methodology as a form of socially engineering the public at large, and the most cogent revelation about this experimentation is that they touted an average 71% success rate in their experimentation. This suggests that the overall mass mind-control experimentation had a much farther reach than just mental institutions and prisons, with measurable results. How this was done will be discussed in the next chapter.

A recent article published by *The Sun* newspaper in the UK entitled, *SPY SECRETS Truth about CIA's illegal MKUltra mind-control experiments – using drugs, hypnosis and electronic devices- revealed in sensational new documents officials hid for decades,* was published on Dec. 7, 2018. The link to the article is below, or it can be looked up by the title for those interested in recent information revealed through Freedom of Information

(FOIA) requests sought for 20 years and obtained by John Greenwald, Jr. and reported to *The Sun*.

<https://www.thesun.co.uk/news/7920010/cia-mkultra-mind-control-drugs-hypnosis-electric-documents/>

The most important element I want the reader to focus on is not the experiments performed by the CIA in mental institutions or on prisoners with LSD and other drugs, or even through implanting electrodes (all of which they did), but to focus on what methodology they may have used against the public that yielded such a high average success rate. This will be explained more as we progress in this presentation.

The fact is, as I revealed in depth in *The Psychology of Becoming Human*, that many methods of psychological control were used against the public from the earliest years of the 20th century onward. In that book I proved beyond the shadow of a doubt that psychology was being abused to sway the public's buying habits through investigating what colors were most appealing to people in newspaper and magazine ads, what shapes were the most appealing, what would catch the eye of potential buyers, and how best to trick the public into buying the products that sellers wanted sold through abuse of psychologically manipulating the public to boost their sales. This form of psychological manipulation has turned into a highly refined science as advertising has advanced from print to radio to television and movies into the modern internet deluge of incessant advertising. The desire to control the mind of the buying public has only become more sophisticated as technology has advanced, but the purpose is and has always been controlling the mind of the public.

Advertising is only one example of what the nephew of Sigmund Freud, Edward Bernays, coined as Public Relations in his book entitled *Propaganda* published in 1928. Through continual psychological manipulation every society worldwide has been subliminally manipulated in their buying habits, their political beliefs, their religious beliefs and everything else. Every culture has been sold a psychological perceptual illusion, a false perception of reality, totally based on manipulating your emotions to deliver a desired result for those who seek to shape and control your mind.

In recent times it has come to light that Facebook has performed subversive psychological experiments on their clients without their knowledge or consent. This abuse was finally uncovered, and Facebook was forced to admit this illegal and secret psychological manipulation. To date, Facebook has not been prosecuted for this massive psychological experiment on the public mind. On the heels of the 2018 midterm elections in the USA, it has now come to light that wealthy Democrat operatives paid to have false Russian bots created to work a negative internet campaign of lies against a Republican candidate in one of the most glaring cases of voter fraud to come to light. Whether the perpetrators are brought to justice over this psychological manipulation to sway voters away from voting for the targeted Republican politician remains to be seen. The target candidate did lose the election based on this form of subversive political psychological warfare, and that is what it is, psychological warfare.

Wikipedia defines Psychological Warfare this way, in part:

> *"Psychological warfare (PSYWAR), or the basic aspects of modern psychological operations (PSYOP), have been known by many other names or terms, including MISO, Psy Ops, political warfare, "Hearts and Minds", and propaganda. The term is used "to denote any action which is practiced mainly by psychological methods* **with the aim of evoking a planned psychological reaction in other people". Various techniques are used, and are aimed at influencing a target audience's value system, belief system, <u>emotions</u>, motives, reasoning, or behavior. It is used to induce confessions or reinforce attitudes and behaviors favorable to the originator's objectives, and are sometimes combined with black operations or false flag tactics.** *It is also used to destroy the morale of enemies through tactics that aim to depress troops' psychological states. Target audiences can be governments, organizations, groups, and individuals, and is not just limited to soldiers. Civilians of foreign territories can also be targeted* **by technology and media** *so as to cause an effect in the government of their country.*

When reading these explanations, one must realize that to demoralize an enemy you have to hit them on the emotional level. Information of any nature in and of itself used to sway a target population does no good whatsoever if you can't hit them on an emotional level. This applies to everything from advertising to religious and political beliefs. To manipulate a target population is not solely dependent on demoralizing, for mood-elevating propaganda works equally as effectively as demoralizing emotions. In fact, as the adage goes, it is easier to attract flies with sugar than with vinegar. As will be seen, it is easier to lure target populations into cognitive mind control traps through hopes and good feelings than it is to always use negative emotion to sway them. Make no mistake, every means of emotional control is used to push selected human herds to go straight down the paths their emotions can lead them. To think that you are not manipulable through such subversive means, or that you are somehow immune from such subtle emotional psychological manipulation only leaves you susceptible to this type of psychological abuse. Denying this is taking place only makes you an easier target.

Through manipulation of our emotions, as noted in chapter one, we are all guilty of manipulating others around us through similar tactics, whether we want to admit it or not. Each of us has desires and all of us are guilty of using emotional manipulation against our loved ones and our acquaintances to get what we want out of them. The manner we each may use for this emotional manipulation may vary from person to person, but everyone does it, and has it done to them in return. Where experts in mind control excel is in knowing this fact and also knowing how to sway mass perceptions through similar emotional manipulation as a psychological weapon.

Although I have cited some of the most recent examples with the SPR psychologists and the Fabian Society, controlling human consciousness goes back thousands of years, whether it was defined and refined into the soft science of Psychology or not. Controlling the human herds has always been within the purview of a select group of elite controllers for at least the last 6,000 years of recorded human history. Accepting this one fact alone may be a large pill for some readers to swallow, but it is inarguably true if one but studies history in the correct light to see it. I will provide many examples to support this contention so the reader can come to their own conclusions as we move forward.

Returning to the Wikipedia explanations about psychological warfare, I must sidetrack briefly to expose what is meant by false flag operations. One of the best ways to manipulate herds is to create an incident and then spark either indignation or a fervor for revenge to drive nations into war. One of the prime examples of a historical false flag operation was the sinking of the Lusitania, which was a contrived event, that finally led the U.S. to get involved in WW I when the nation was not interested in participating in just another European conflict.

The Lusitania was the largest passenger ship in the world at that time. It was illegally loaded with munitions and war goods bound for the United Kingdom, yet the passengers on the ship were unaware of the fact that the ship was carrying arms and ammunition which made it a target for German U-boats. Although the German Embassy printed warnings in 50 newspapers, the Lusitania embarked on its voyage to England with 128 passengers from the United States on board on May 1, 1915. Six days later on May 7, the Lusitania was near the coast of Ireland when it was discovered by a German U-boat that torpedoed the Lusitania, which sparked an explosion inside the ship from the armaments it carried, and the ship sank with many casualties.

Although it did take two years to drag the reluctant United States into the First World War, the sinking of the Lusitania was the emotional false flag catalyst that was used to inflame American passions to get involved in a war that only two years previously they were not remotely interested in participating. A similar false flag operation was perpetrated by the United States government at the hands of the FDR administration which pushed the Japanese into bombing Pearl Harbor. Roosevelt had information that the attack was coming but left the majority of the American fleet anchored at Pearl Harbor knowing it was a sitting duck for a Japanese attack. After WW I, the Americans were equally reluctant to get involved in another European conflict, so another catalyst was needed to galvanize the American public into a war furor to get the U.S. into WW II. The attack on Pearl Harbor was the false flag operation that finally sparked enough horror and emotional anger and self-righteous emotions of being victimized in a surprise attack, and America was once again dragged into a war not of its choosing, but which was manipulated by elite controllers who knew how to sway public opinion and who had no problem murdering others to fulfill a profiteering war agenda.

In any false flag-type operation, the primary focus of the attack is to shock the psyche of the public. This initially creates a stunned, emotionally numbing effect, just like we lived through with the 9/11 attacks. Once people recover from the initial emotional and psychological shock, the emotional outrage begins, and any country is only steps away from stepping into a war footing seeking retaliation against the perpetrators. This is how false flag operations can be used to throw nations, in fact the entire world, into war.

These are just some major false flag operations that we have been subjected to in the last century. In other centuries, another example of the false flag operation is the Affair of the

Diamond Necklace used against Marie Antionette, which was a fabricated propaganda lie to begin with, but which was used to stir up discontent by the French masses that eventually led to the French Revolution and Marie's ultimate beheading by the mob.

In every instance, the false flag is perpetrated to incite emotional discord in the target population. The elite controllers of this planet have no regard for those whose lives they throw away if their business is in banking and making war profits, or simply seeking political power. To these elite psychopaths, humanity is nothing but disposable herds, there only to serve as fodder to their whims and desires. Again, this is a truth that some reader's minds will rebel at, but there is more than enough historical evidence, once researched, that verifies all of this. This explains the value of false flags and false narratives in psychologically moving the human herds by manipulating their emotions to do things they are otherwise reluctant to do – like go to war.

Once the public gets past the initial cognitive shock of a false flag operation, like Hitler's burning of the Reichstag or a 9/11 event, their emotions turn to revenge on the parties who are blamed for the false flag event. Human emotions are utterly predictable with false flag shock operations. All it takes is a demagogue to point the human herd in the direction sought, someone with a megaphone to 'rally the troops' and wrap them in indignant patriotism, and war is half a step away. These tactics have been used time and again over the ages and the human herds always react the same. The first reaction is fear as the event is taking place if the false flag incident is an act of violence. The greater the carnage, the greater the fear and psychological shock.

Out of fear comes that desire for payback and the rallying for patriotism is next in line to go get the bastards that did the dirty deed. Every one of these facets of a false flag operation generates these kinds of predictable emotional reactions. We have seen it time and again and it works every time with the majority of the human herds, regardless of where they are in the world. Turning the herds in the direction the controllers want them to go does not require capturing the imagination of every individual, you only need to capture the minds of the majority to steer the herd down the road you want to take them.

For some explanations on how crowd psychology works, let's take a look at some of what Gustave Le Bon wrote with his observations about the crowd when he posited his theory in *The Crowd* in 1895:

> *"The disappearance of conscious personality and **the turning of feelings and thoughts in a definite direction**, which are the primary characteristics of a crowd about to become organised, do not always involve the simultaneous presence of a number of individuals on one spot. **Thousands of isolated individuals may acquire at certain moments, and under the influence of certain violent emotions — such, for example, as a great national event — the characteristics of a psychological crowd.** It will be sufficient in that case that a mere chance should bring them together for their acts to at once*

*assume the characteristics peculiar to the acts of a crowd. At certain moments half a dozen men might constitute a psychological crowd, which may not happen in the case of hundreds of men gathered together by accident. On the other hand, **an entire nation, though there may be no visible agglomeration, may become a crowd under the action of certain influences**."*

*"The most striking peculiarity presented by a psychological crowd is the following: Whoever be the individuals that compose it, however like or unlike be their mode of life, their occupations, their character, or their intelligence, the fact that they have been transformed into a crowd puts them in possession of a sort of collective mind which makes them feel, think, and act in a manner quite different from that in which each individual of them would feel, think, and act were he in a state of isolation. There are certain ideas and feelings which do not come into being, or do not transform themselves into acts except in the case of individuals forming a crowd. **The psychological crowd is a provisional being formed of heterogeneous elements, which for a moment are combined, exactly as the cells which constitute a living body form by their reunion a new being which displays***

characteristics very different from those possessed by each of the cells singly."

"A crowd is not merely impulsive and mobile. Like a savage, it is not prepared to admit that anything can come between its desire and the realisation of its desire. It is the less capable of understanding such an intervention, in consequence of the feeling of irresistible power given it by its numerical strength. The notion of impossibility disappears for the individual in a crowd. An isolated individual knows well enough that alone he cannot set fire to a palace or loot a shop, and should he be tempted to do so, he will easily resist the temptation. **Making part of a crowd, he is conscious of the power given him by number, and it is sufficient to suggest to him ideas of murder or pillage for him to yield immediately to temptation. An unexpected obstacle will be destroyed with frenzied rage.** *Did the human organism allow of the perpetuity of furious passion, it might be said that the normal condition of a crowd baulked in its wishes is just such a state of furious passion."*

[Bold emphasis mine]

In reading these passages, I ask the reader to take note of recent events in the U.S. where unruly mobs of SJW's or Antifa activists turn into screaming mobs, pounding on the doors of the Supreme Court building; or chanting trite, contrived slogans in cadence exhibiting their solidarity, and intimidating innocent passers-by on city streets. These are mobs, and the observations that Le Bon makes in regard to mobs or crowds turning into a single-brained entity of its own lowered mob intelligence should be noted in these actions.

As Le Bon observed, to form a crowd, there doesn't have to be a gathering of people in a single locale, but that a galvanizing event like Pearl Harbor or 9/11 can generate the same crowd mentality of a singular intelligence with one goal in mind. This type of psychological crowd manipulation is used on the larger scale by the Fabian Communists worldwide today. To create a crowd, one can do so with political instigation and propaganda where a certain political or religious segment of the population that feels victimized can easily be prompted into violence once the crowd mentality is drilled into the psyche of the target audience. Victimization is very effective for creating sentiments of righteous indignation over some presumed injustice that creates the victimhood psychological mindset. Victims are always driven by emotion and are easily turned into a mob with little to no instigation. All it takes is a skilled agitator to amplify the victim mindset to turn people into a destructive and violent mob animal. We see this on the streets in the U.S. and we are starting to see similar actions with agitators embedded in the Yellow Vest movement in Europe.

Just using Le Bon's examples, one might argue that emotional manipulation is only theoretical where it comes to mind control and crowd psychology because he was only positing the theory based on his observations. To shut down any argument of that nature, let's take a look at one of the dastardliest people who turned Le Bon's 'theory' into actual application. The following passages are from Adolf Hitler's *Mein Kampf:*

> *"Propaganda must always address itself to the broad masses of the people. (...) All propaganda must be presented in a popular form* **and must fix its intellectual level so as not to be above the heads of the least intellectual of those to whom it is directed.** *(...) The art of propaganda consists precisely in being able to awaken the imagination of the public* **through an appeal to their <u>feelings</u>,** *in finding the appropriate psychological form that will arrest the attention and appeal to the hearts of the national masses.* **The broad masses of the people are not made up of diplomats or professors of public jurisprudence nor simply of persons who are able to form reasoned judgment in given cases, but a vacillating crowd of human children who are constantly wavering between one idea and another.** *(...) The great majority of a nation is so feminine in its character and outlook that* **its thought and conduct are ruled by sentiment rather than by sober reasoning. This sentiment, however, is not complex, but simple and**

consistent. It is not highly differentiated, but has only the negative and positive notions of love and hatred, right and wrong, truth and falsehood."

"Propaganda must not investigate the truth objectively and, in so far as it is favourable to the other side, **present it according to the theoretical rules of justice;** *yet it must present only that aspect of the truth which is favourable to its own side. (...)* **The receptive powers of the masses are very restricted, and their understanding is feeble. On the other hand, they quickly forget. Such being the case, all effective propaganda must be confined to a few bare essentials and those must be expressed as far as possible in stereotyped formulas. These** <u>**slogans**</u> **should be persistently repeated until the very last individual has come to grasp the idea that has been put forward. (...) Every change that is made in the subject of a propagandist message must always emphasize the same conclusion. The leading slogan must of course be illustrated in many ways and from several angles, but in the end one must always return to the assertion of the same formula."**

[Bold emphasis mine]

Although these words were written by Hitler, Hitler was a Socialist and operated from the same standpoint of propaganda used by all Communists/Socialists. If one looks at the mainstream media of the Left in the U.S. today, they do not see news reporting, they see propaganda and sloganeering as just elucidated by Hitler in 1925. The primary slogan of the Left today in America is 'Destroy Trump!' The daily mantra is 'social justice' and the major media networks all read from the same script using the same words to galvanize their brainwashed social justice parrots into lockstep and groupthink, whose membership only echoes the phrases mouthed by the leftist media and politicians thinking that they have the measure of reality. These brainwashed, indoctrinated parrots to the Marxist cause are simply wind-up toys, mobs who are enslaved to the propaganda of their particular political ideology, all victims and all emotionally outraged over presumed harms perpetrated against their self-deluded victimhood. The mob is locked and loaded and emotionally ready to be triggered into violence when the right event comes along to send them into the streets to wreak havoc and destruction upon any who do not agree with their creed or victim status.

But don't be dismayed, the Left doesn't have the corner on the market of righteous indignation and victimhood. The Right-wing media plays against the opposition's emotions using God and Guns as their motto, emotionally manipulating people into a false sense of patriotism against those godless commies. No one is immune from the psychological emotional manipulation, regardless of how they protest that they are not victims. The evidence is glaringly apparent, and it is only those who feel threatened and victimized that are the most psychologically malleable to this type of mind control. You may hide behind ego bravado and scream you are not mind-controlled, but I will beg to differ based on a mountain of evidence in plain sight that proves otherwise.

3. Operation Mockingbird

The full scope for understanding emotional mind control can't be understood until the public is aware of the CIA's Operation Mockingbird. We must remember that it was the CIA's MK-Ultra mind-control experimentation that, once revealed, caused such a public uproar.

Operation Mockingbird was the CIA's endeavor to control public perceptions through control of the media. What goes widely unreported to the public, even today, is that Operation Mockingbird, or Project Mockingbird as it was referred to in the agency, was a domestic propaganda project to shape public opinion through controlling the news media and what the public was allowed to know. Although the CIA claimed to have shut down the program in 1976, there is little doubt that it is still ongoing, and that the CIA is working as a disinformation service for the Fabian Globalists seeking to undermine the United States government, particularly the Trump administration.

The former head of the CIA, John Brennan, was fired by President Trump, as was the head of the DIA, James Clapper. Both these men have also had their security clearances revoked and are now working as commentators for the Left-wing media continually seeking to undermine a duly elected American president. During the U.S. Senate Church Committee hearings, testimony was given by William Schap that stated:

"About a third of the whole CIA budget went to media propaganda operations... We're talking about hundreds of millions of dollars a year just for that... close to a billion dollars are being spent every year by the United States on secret propaganda."

The Church Committee also discovered:

"The CIA currently maintains a network of several hundred foreign individuals around the world who provide intelligence for the CIA and at times attempt to influence opinion through the use of covert propaganda. These individuals provide the CIA with direct access to a large number of newspapers and periodicals, scores of press services and news agencies, radio and television stations, commercial book publishers, and other foreign media outlets."

This funneling of cash and CIA operatives placed within media outlets is even more pronounced today than it was back in the 1970s when the Church Committee held its hearings. We also have 'ex-CIA' agents holding positions in the U.S. House and Senate, as well as being 'reporters' of the news in the mainstream media, and by this author's estimation, none of them can be trusted to look out for American interests.

The control of the media, publishing houses, commercial book publishers as well as textbook publishers, and now the internet by the CIA presents an inherent threat to the public being honestly informed of any issues that go against the Globalist Communist agenda. Through the subversive use of what is known as controlled opposition, all media is being abused to push forward an agenda of disinformation and emotional psychological programming that keeps the public uninformed worldwide and left to make their political or religious decisions based on blatant disinformation. No one can possibly make an informed decision on most matters when they are being fed a constant diet of political disinformation which has also permeated the school systems at all levels.

There is no avenue of American life that has not been influenced by such disinformation tactics to control the minds and perceptions of the public. Prior to the establishment of the State of Israel (which happened in collusion between the political Zionists and the Fabian Communists), American churches were infiltrated, mostly evangelicals, and sold the bill of goods that the establishment of the State of Israel would be a fulfillment of prophecy forecasted in the Bible. All too many American Christians bought this lie based on their religious beliefs, and a bunch of Communist Eastern European gangs (the Stern Gang and the Irgun) placed themselves in Israel in positions of power and created the Jewish State. Naturally, Christian evangelicals whose eyes were focused on Heaven and the ultimate return of Jesus based on this fabricated illusion that the establishment of the State of Israel was Bible prophecy, are still blindly following the Communist State of Israel believing it is God's Kingdom. Throughout this perceptual cognitive charade, there was no information provided to the American Christian public that revealed this lie, and to this day most Christians still believe the false prophetic lie. This serves to bolster blind support for the State of Israel in the American evangelical churches to this day and has been the cause of every Middle Eastern conflict since Israel was established.

In earlier times there were hundreds of different newspaper outlets and many different sources of investigative reporting where Americans and others could get their news and form their opinions. Through Fabian-controlled corporate consolidation for over a century, these varied voices have been bought out, forced out of business or consolidated into a vast global media empire that now serves as a Fabian propaganda mechanism more than it delivers news. We have the CIA and Project Mockingbird to thank for this.

The choice of the word Mockingbird should not go unnoticed in this project's naming. Wikipedia tells us about *Mockingbirds*:

> *"Mockingbirds are a group of New World passerine birds from the Mimidae family. They are best known for the habit of some species **mimicking the songs of other birds and the sounds of insects and amphibians**, often loudly*

and in rapid succession. There are about 17 species in three genera. These do not appear to form a monophyletic lineage: Mimus and Nesomimus are quite closely related; their closest living relatives appear to be thrashers, such as the sage thrasher. Melanotis is more distinct; it seems to represent a very ancient basal lineage of Mimidae.

*The only mockingbird commonly found in North America is the northern mockingbird (Mimus polyglottos). The Greek word polyglottos means **multiple languages.** "*

[Bold emphasis mine]

It is not by accident that the CIA chose this word or this bird as its operational mascot, as the mockingbird is a mimic. It can deceive other birds with its mimicked calls and is intimately suitable to name an operation for disinformation where data may 'look like and smell like' news, but is actually a counterfeit, pretending to be something it isn't. When you listen to the vast majority of mainstream TV news, you will hear one reporter after another from network to network using the same words and phrases any given day if you switch from channel to channel, and they all mimic the propaganda messages passed down by the two leading news supplying agencies AP (Associated Press) and UPI (United Press International). These are the two primary news feed sources used in the U.S. today, and their reach is global.

Through such total and contrived news sourcing and control, the world is fed a perceptual illusion designed by the Mockingbird press. Sadly, all too many people still rely on and believe these propaganda outlets are trustworthy. The fact that they are not is why President Trump constantly assaults these news outlets as Fake News, because he is fully aware of this Globalist/CIA propaganda network. With current accusations and verifiably provable manipulation, shadow banning and outright censorship of any information that does not support the Globalist Communist left-wing narrative by the tech super-giants – Google, Facebook and Twitter – the control over the flow of information is only expanding in the Trump era. Any conservative voice of opposition is being quashed electronically by these tech giants, so the public is only fed one narrative – the narrative of Globalist Marxist Communism.

One of the primary and most effective tactics of brainwashing, or mind control, is repetition. The more one is subjected to repetitious ideas day in and day out, they start to believe the lies because they are incessantly repeated as real. When one can't move from one news outlet to the next without hearing the same repetitious diatribe (such as hate Trump), then they become subject to the mind control of the repetitive assault on their consciousness through emotional control. None of the so-called news these days is sterile of emotional bile from either side. All outlets that present the news work against one's emotions to sell their papers or get people to tune into their broadcasts. These outlets serve to push the individual's hot buttons and we now live in a climate of hatred from all sides with emotional psychological manipulation being the primary weapon for abuse used by all media outlets.

We are programmed to pay attention to the foolish antics and affairs of meaningless Hollywood personalities, and we are expected to give the Communist opinions of the Hollywood Left credence when they are in fact just another group of subversive operatives put in place to destroy a nation from within through propaganda. Sadly, too many people fall for this cult of personality and their star-stunned belief in their idols makes them that much more susceptible to emotional manipulation when these people who 'pretend to be other people' to make a living spout their political opinions. We are bombarded through film and radio with an incessant drumbeat of propaganda and it is all designed to rile us up emotionally so one side or the other cannot only gain market share but keep our nations in conflict within their own borders.

Divide and conquer has always been the rule of the day for Communists to destroy a target nation from within, and in the U.S. today, we are sitting at ground zero on this type of emotionally and psychologically fragmenting a nation until it self-destructs. We are seeing the same thing starting to advance itself in Europe with the Yellow Vest movement seeking to stop the Globalism of the EU with nations trying to retain their eroding sovereignty, and the constant fight with the Globalists stalling and seeking to overturn the will of the British voters in the Brexit mess. The rise of Populism is a push-back by some nation states like Brazil, Poland and Italy, yet even populist movements are driven through emotional manipulation.

All of this goes back to Le Bon's defining an ages-old means to control cultures and solidifying it into an identifiable doctrine – Crowd Psychology. What we are observing today with the conflict of political ideologies in the U.S. can be fully equated with how Christianity did the same thing with the Pagan statues and edifices of old as what the Left is doing by pulling down Confederate war statues in the U.S. There is not one whit of difference in the mentality of emotionally riled and self-righteous crowds seeking to destroy the past and rewrite history in their likeness when you objectively compare these events. We have seen the same emotional manipulation as the basis for every 'revolution' that ever happened in human history, whether it was the Affair of the Diamond Necklace that led to the French Revolution, or the revolution against Rome with the Bar Kochba revolt in Israel when the Jews believed Simon Bar Kochba to be the prophesied Jewish messiah. Pick any revolution you choose from the tapestry of human history and you will find emotional psychological manipulation at its root – bar none!

4. Control Through Fear and Terror

The most drastic manner to control any large population is through fear, terror and intimidation. Human history is rife with atrocities committed by tyrants, everyone from Roman emperors to Genghis Khan to the Huns, Hitler, Lenin, Stalin and Mao. Ugly as it is, terrorism works as a very effective form of crowd control. Fear is one of the most basic elements of the human emotional spectrum and it is very easy to exploit by those who have no scruples in performing terrorist acts to 'shock and awe' their target populations into compliance. Fear has worked time and again over the ages to subdue the masses, so its effectiveness cannot be denied where it comes to defining one of the strongest weapons for emotional manipulation to control large populations of humans.

Fear is what drives human emotions on the most rudimentary level and lies at the root of the fight or flight mechanism. Fear is instinctual in all forms of life since it is tied into the very survival of every physical form. No one escapes fear programming in the physical form on the most fundamental level, it is a program that is hard-coded into every living thing. As this book progresses there will be deeper discussion on how fear rules our consciousness beyond the physical survival level, but for now I want to provide some instances of how tyrants use fear when they come to power to enslave entire populations, and it has been a very effective weapon over the millennia to keep populations in check in many forms.

As much as you may personally protest this concept at this stage of reading this book, it will be revealed that the human psyche is governed more by fear than any other emotion, and that includes love and hate. Through a continual process of negative reinforcement throughout our lives, fear takes the driver's seat in virtually every decision we make on the deepest level of our emotional landscape. Our parents start out as the primary punishment givers, and this is elevated into the school systems where we are basically brainwashed into accepting and being tested for how accurately we have digested the course work and our cultural myths, particularly where our presumed history is concerned. Through the constant threat of failure, the fear mechanism gets deeply ingrained in our habits over the course of 12 years of primary schooling through persistent negative reinforcement. We are taught to toe the line or take a failing grade if we challenge what we are taught. Cultures around the world are structured in a similar manner and fear is the major controller of the mind in such environments ruled by negative reinforcement. The fear of failure ensures that the brainwashing works very effectively.

One of the greatest fears that ruled consciousness in the ancient world was the fear of famine. It is not widely reported in our school course material, but the Roman Empire during the reign of the Caesars was a quasi-socialist state, with government-sponsored bread giveaways to keep the population quelled.

During times of famine when the bread dole was interrupted, and people went into a state of hunger and privation, revolts by the dependent classes and slaves were soon to follow, and violence in the streets erupted periodically during bouts of food shortages in those ages. In the year 90, the historian Diodorus reported on one of these times of food privation in a battle between Romans and Italians over the harvest:

> *"Since the ripe ears were there before them ready to be reaped, they settled with their blood the question who was to have the essential food. No one waited on the urging of his commander. Nature itself, confronting them with the cold logic of deprivation, spurred them on to bravery. Each man stoutly faced the prospect of dying by the sword because he feared death by privation."*

Although natural famines are frightening enough, in our world today we have manufactured famines by the Globalist elite. As much as you may be shocked by such a straightforward statement, famine serves a dual purpose to the elite world controllers. On one hand its serves as a population control mechanism to kill off the unnecessary and weak 'useless eaters', usually the young and aged, and through forced deprivation it raises the cost of goods so their corporate enterprises can rake in huge profits from the artificially-induced food shortages. When dealing with the Globalist Communists we must realize that control of the masses is ever important, and that includes controlling the population and culling the human herds through whatever means can be found to keep their tyranny functioning, whether that be by war or famine.

Controlling the world food supply is a major goal of the Globalist agenda. Through corporations like Monsanto, they have produced single-generation hybrid seeds that only grow one crop, and if a farmer wants to grow another crop, they have to purchase the single-generation seeds from Monsanto to keep their farming business going. We have to ask why anyone other than a psychopath would dream up a scheme to take control over the world food supply this way and hold it hostage for financial gain rather than continue to use natural seed stock that can generate new crops from grown seed stock indefinitely. It is from our past with unpredictable famines that humanity has a hidden fear of 'not-enoughness'. None of us in the modern world knows the origin of this inner anxiety, but it is ever-present after thousands of generations of humanity living on the edge of uncertainty as to where their next meal may come from.

Terror has always been a weapon. It is used to the advantage of terrorists as a psychological weapon in the modern era with bloodthirsty ISIS terrorists, MS-13 gang members and drug cartel enforcers, and it has been used strategically as a weapon by conquerors to shock the conscious of a target population and cow them into submission through fear of survival. Terror is designed to make one's enemies capitulate because of the horror that wars driven by terror spawn. If the deeds perpetrated are terrible enough, the consciousness of the targeted population will be stunned by the horror of it all and will willing surrender rather than die such horrible deaths fighting the conquering armies. The more bloodthirsty and callous the terror tactics are, the more the emotional shock value to the psyche of a population that has never seen such horror.

Although Dracula has come down to the modern world through the legend of the vampire from the 1897 Bram Stoker horror novel, the real Count Dracula is considered a national hero in his homeland. Vlad III of Wallachia lived in the 15th century and by some accounts saved Europe from the Ottoman hordes. Vlad Dracula saved Europe from Ottoman conquest by using terror to strike fear into his Ottoman enemies by impaling his adversaries on tall stakes to strike terror into his enemies. He was also a capable warrior. Many legends surround Vlad the Impaler, some perhaps fanciful, but his reputation for cruelty seems to go unchallenged. The reputation of his callous brutality and his willingness to impale his enemies did strike terror in the ranks of the Ottomans. This is but one example of how terror can be used for a more positive purpose, although I don't personally sanction Vlad's tactics.

Genghis Kahn and his Mongol army were indiscriminate murdering invaders, killing warriors and civilians alike. His armies reportedly piled up pyramids of the skulls of their victims and it is reported that Genghis Khan made Attila the Hun look like an amateur in comparison. Although the Mongols killed hundreds of thousands, they were not big on torture but instead delivered quick deaths. Their reputation of fear was due to the fact that once a city was targeted for revenge for failure to capitulate to Mongol demands, there were few, if any survivors.

The Seljuk Turks had a city called Merv which was a rich city of education, libraries, palaces and observatories. Genghis Khan sent emissaries to the city in 1218 and demanded tribute and women, which the Seljuks not only refused, but they also killed Khan's messengers. Three years later the Mongol army arrived at the city gate and demanded tribute once again and demanded that the city surrender. This time the Turks complied, but because Genghis Khan's messengers were killed before, the Mongols massacred the entire city's inhabitants and, as some legends report, each Mongol soldier was ordered to behead 300-400 civilians and then burn the city down. This was how Genghis Khan and his armies dealt with double-dealers and those who refused to capitulate to his demands. His descendants were not much better. So much for capitulation to terrorists.

Most of the people in the West are fully informed of Hitler's 6 million Jews being killed in the Holocaust. What goes unreported in the Fabian Communist-controlled education system is that in comparison to Hitler's 6 million, the Communists make Hitler look like an amateur. I am by no means sanctioning or defending what Hitler did with the Holocaust, but people do not understand that nothing happens in a vacuum. What also goes widely unreported in the history books is that one of the main reasons Hitler had problems with the Jews is that they were the major proponents of Communism in Germany at that time, and it was also during this period that the Communist organization Antifa came into being. Yes, the same Antifa organization of thugs now prowling the streets of America spouting Communist slogans. Hitler's Brown Shirts were involved in frequent street brawls with the Communist Antifa thugs. So, the reader must understand that much of Hitler's problem with the Jews also had to do with their Communist leanings as much as anything else. This part of the story has been intentionally expunged from Western history books because it doesn't fit the Fabian Communist narrative of those 'evil Nazis'.

What also goes untaught in our classrooms is that probably the greatest mass murderer of all time was a Communist Jew named Lazar Kaganovich. This mass murderer, who committed some of the worst crimes against humanity, was allowed to die of old age in Russia without ever being brought to justice for his crimes. Kaganovich is single-handedly responsible for the deaths of 12 million Ukrainians through formulated famine in an event known as the Holodomor. It is the greatest act of genocide in the 20th century. But you may draw some minor comfort from the fact that he was tried posthumously almost 20 years after his death and found guilty of genocide. One can only imagine the fear and terror of the Ukrainian people as they slowly starved to death and knowing it was being perpetrated on purpose. But we are only allowed to know about Hitler's 6 million and the Holocaust industry has shoved it down our throats incessantly for seventy years. We never hear a whisper about Kaganovich. How odd.

Lazar Kaganovich was responsible for this Holodomor famine under the brutal Stalinist regime in 1932-1933. Stalin is known for being responsible for the murder of millions using his famous show trials to convict and execute, or send to die in the gulag, any and all adversaries to the Communist ideology and Stalin's dictatorial policies. This also goes widely unreported in

Western schools and university systems while Hitler is constantly held up as the evilest man of the 20th century to Western school children.

Just as most people are unaware of the existence of the British Fabian Society, they are equally unaware of the fact that one of the early members of the Fabian Society, George Bernard Shaw, was enthralled with Joe Stalin and felt that his murderous model of Communist tyranny in Russia represented the New World Order the Fabians were trying to create. If you want to know the Fabian Society's plan for the Western world through masquerading their murderous doctrine with the word Globalism, then let there be no doubt what the true agenda will be for humanity is if it isn't stopped. Under Communist rule in Russia, we find 100 million dead. How does Hitler's 6 million sound in comparison now?

Let's now take a look at Communist China under Mao Tse Tung. From 1958 to 1962 Mao initiated his Great Leap Forward initiative which eventually led to the deaths of 45 million people making it the biggest single episode of mass murder in history. Here again, famine became the weapon as millions died from faulty Communist policies. Along with policies such as this, many Leftists in the West laud Mao with eliminating opium addiction in China. Naturally these advocates fail to relate the fact that Mao's cure for drug addiction was a bullet to the back of the head. Within only three short years after Mao's rise to power with the Communist Party, where there were once 70 million opium growers, users and addicts, there were none left alive. Problem solved.

So, let's analyze briefly here; in Russia under Communist tyranny, we have over 100 million dead. In Communist China we have almost 115 million or more dead through starvation or outright murder, just like in Russia. We have to ask why we only hear incessantly about the 6 million of the Holocaust and Hitler and not a whisper about over 200 million dead at the hands of international Communism. What's wrong with this picture?

Wherever Communists thrive, even under the presumed benevolent front of Socialism, tyranny always follows. Fear and terrorism are the weapons of choice, the people are simply fodder tossed into the grist mill for destruction. Human beings are disposable goods to these self-appointed elite Globalist controllers. Welcome to reality. Fear rules. Fear controls the masses.

Another weapon in the arsenal of fear used by kings, tyrants and governments throughout time is the law. To be fair and honest, the West has not been totally innocent where abuses of power are concerned, but it chooses to hide behind laws to do its dirty work as its force for fear and control of the masses. Admittedly, every civilization that ever existed had its laws, but the illusion in the West in the modern world is that law is about justice. Law is not about justice; it is about fear and retribution. It is just tyranny put into a nice-sounding package and it is only another perceptual illusion. The law is masquerading as something it isn't. Laws are just another means of social control through fear.

Law is a velvet covered hammer, nothing more and nothing less. As an example, I will share a little bit about what is known these days as the *Bloody Code* from Wikipedia:

> *""Bloody Code" is a term used to refer to the system of crimes and punishments in England in the 18th and early 19th centuries. It was not referred to as such in its own time, but the name was given later owing to the sharply increased number of people given the death penalty, even for crimes considered minor by today's society.*

> *In 1688 there were 50 offences on the statute book punishable by death, but that number had almost quadrupled by 1776, and it reached 220 by the end of the century. Most of the new laws introduced during that period were concerned with the defence of property, which some commentators have interpreted as a form of class suppression of the poor by the rich. George Savile, 1st Marquess of Halifax, expressed a contemporary view when he said that "Men are not hanged for stealing horses, but that horses may not be stolen". Grand larceny was one of the crimes that drew the death penalty; it was defined as the theft of goods worth more than 12 pence, about one-twentieth of the weekly wage for a skilled worker at the time. As the 18th century proceeded, jurors often deliberately*

under-assessed the value of stolen goods, in order to avoid a mandatory death sentence."

"Jurist William Blackstone said of the Bloody Code:

It is a melancholy truth, that among the variety of actions which men are daily liable to commit, no less than a hundred and sixty have been declared by Act of Parliament to be felonious without benefit of clergy; or, in other words, to be worthy of instant death."

There was some action against the Bloody Laws seeking an alternative method of deterrent, and one was compelling people into the slavery of indentured servitude. As should be obvious from the foregoing passages, law is not about justice, it is about the appearance of justice while actually being punishment or retribution. Belief in the law is just another perceptual illusion through which societies are controlled. Law is a *weapon.*

This reliance on legal vengeance in the West goes back to biblical tenets and the laws handed down by the Jewish God. That is the foundation of Western jurisprudence regardless of how anyone, Left or Right, wants to argue to the contrary. Although most believing Christians think there is only the 10 Commandments in the Bible, there are actually 613 Commandments passed down by the God of the Old Testament.

Jehovah was a real stickler when it came to having his people obey His commands.

The bloodthirstiness of the God of the Old Testament has translated into modern laws, but our modern laws are not based on old Common Law where an offense had to be perpetrated before an act could be tried. These days, based on the corruption of Fabian-oriented bureaucratic administrative laws, most of us are potential felons when we walk out our doors in the morning. These days, laws have even less to do with justice than they did before, even during the age of the Bloody Laws. Today law is used as a weapon just in case you *might* commit an offense against the State. We are fined and penalized, not because we perpetrated a crime, but because we *might* perpetrate a crime. With Communistic bureaucratic zoning laws and other manufactured offenses, our freedoms are continually eroded away as States dream up more ways to steal our livelihood that only a psychopathic Communist can imagine. When the goal is the destruction of the working class, State-favored laws to sanction property theft or potential offenses is the rule of the day, not the exception. Through such abuses of the law, the law has become a weapon to be feared, and even without the State to create rules and regulations to hamper our freedoms, we find petty tyrants populating the ranks of Homeowner's Associations from sea to shining sea. As Loki, the arch villain in *The Avengers* movie so accurately stated, "You beg for subjugation." Law is not about justice, it is a weapon of fear to keep the ignorant human crowds under control, and this species has yet to learn that every time they pass a law, we lose a freedom. Every time I hear someone say,

"There ought to be a law," they need to be bitch-slapped, because they are only begging for more tyranny to be used against them. Law is about control, it is not about justice, so stop deceiving yourself that it is.

5. Compassion and Humanitarianism

We are now going to delve into one of the most pernicious and hateful forms of emotional psychological control the world has ever seen, and that is compassion and humanitarianism. These hateful doctrines of mind control are so dangerous because they sound just too nice to be what they actually are as a form of emotional control. I mean, who can argue against compassion and humanitarianism, right? One must be some sort of Grinch to even put these concepts under the microscope and call them tyrannical methods of emotional control, but before this chapter is complete, you will see compassion and humanitarianism in their true light rather than how these emotional manipulations are fed to the public by the truckload day in and day out by both the political Right and Left as they each vie for superiority over who is more compassionate, and this has been done throughout the centuries.

In the East, it is Buddha who is attributed to teaching the doctrine of compassion in roughly the 6th century BC. 500 years later, we find this doctrine of compassion woven into the burgeoning religion of Christianity. Although Buddha is best remembered as a teacher, Jesus is where the doctrine of compassion met with humanitarianism and the compassionate figure of Christ, so the Christian legend goes, when Christ stood up as the defender of the downtrodden. Naturally, Jesus left no written words of his own any more than Buddha did, so all we have is stories told by others who came after them, most who never knew him personally. Was Jesus really this compassionate humanitarian figure that Bible stories and religious propaganda shaped before the canonization of the Bible tells us? We have no real way of knowing, but it does create a feel-good doctrine of behaviors to emulate by the believers of what became the Christian doctrine.

The main doctrine of Christianity didn't sell as well to the Torah-believing Jews as it did to the Gentiles. The God of the Jews played favorites by choosing the Jews above all people as His representatives on Earth. He was also a neurotic and vengeful God who thrived on murder and vengeance, openly advocating theft, rapine and pillage when he ordered the Jews to invade Canaan, as just one example. There is an exquisite dichotomy between the vindictive and neurotic God of the Old Testament and the loving and forgiving God of Jesus. The mental gymnastics required for believers in the Bible to reconcile these glaring differences is astounding, but apologists for the Christian faith have been dancing angels on the head of a pin for centuries trying to justify this glaring contradiction. I am not attacking Christians; I am only stating factually the opposing and contradictory concepts of God presented in their Holy Book. When confronted with these truths, most Christians just shrug and say, "God works in mysterious ways," and the issue is reconciled in their mind by avoiding facing the truth. This type of mental gymnastics and problem avoidance happens with people on so many different subjects that the example just given is only one of multitudes, some of which will be discussed as we continue.

The Christian doctrine, mostly formulated by Paul, an alleged Jewish convert to the belief in Jesus after he had a miraculous vision of Jesus on the Road to Damascus, is a doctrine of submission. The Pauline ideology, which became the foundation of alleged Christianity, is of Roman construction. It instructs people to turn the other cheek; tells slaves to obey their masters; and says render unto Caesar what is Caesar's indicating that everyone should bow to Roman taxation without complaint as they will reap their rewards in some heavenly afterlife dancing around the throne of God and singing his praises forever and ever. That sounds pretty boring to me personally, but it has been sold to Christians since the Roman Jew Paul wrote his treatises and sold them to the Gentile world some 2,000 years ago.

Some people wondered why Paul was so pro-Roman, but the answer is easy to find where in his own writings he claimed to be kin of the 'littlest Herod'. The Herodian family were vassals of Rome, appointed governors by the Roman emperors over the territory in Palestine. They were pro-Roman for some time before Saul/Paul was born into this administrative royal family. This clears up any mystery about Paul's Roman citizenship.

The Hebrews have always been a rebellious lot, even going so far as to rebel against the mandates of their God, so they have a long history of rebelliousness. From the Maccabees to the Bar Kochba revolts, the Jews were a perpetual thorn to Roman rule.

Couple with this information the constant threat of slave revolts, like that of Spartacus around 70 BC, and the Romans needed a doctrine peddled to the masses to create a more submissive populace. Early Christianity was mostly sold to slaves as they were the one target audience that the Roman world wanted disenchanted from any ideas about revolt. The Pauline doctrine, labeled Christianity, filled that need. It promised a utopian afterlife, and part of the terms of attaining that afterlife was adhering to the provisions listed above about submission to their masters, along with a professed belief in Jesus as their savior and messiah. It worked for about 200 years before the doctrine spread and returned to the rebellious nature of its Jewish roots and the Christian mobs did their utmost to destroy the Pagan world and all reminders of it.

The ideological Son of God was a miracle worker, could feed thousands with a few loaves of bread and a few fish, could allegedly walk on water, could heal the blind, deaf and lame, and he was filled with a compassion and humanitarianism that no other mere human could ever hope to match or attain, but which they were expected to emulate. Thus, the submission doctrine of the Roman Jew Paul was coupled with the doctrine of Christ's compassion and pure humanitarianism. "Love thy neighbor as thyself," sounded great preached from the pulpits to a mostly illiterate mass of followers as an ideology, but it rarely translated into the actions of the human believers of the doctrine. Nor did turning the other cheek work out as practicable.

I want to interrupt here for a moment and ask the reader if reading these passages, which are all factual and can be backed up by biblical stories, whether they felt any emotional reaction to my simply revealing facts? Did you find yourself bristling over the information I just shared? And if you felt angry, defensive or challenged by these factual observations, what is your emotional investment in simply facing facts? I attacked no one personally, I only supplied facts about a belief system that is readily verified in the Bible itself. So, if you reacted with negative emotions and jumped to your own defense if you happen to believe the biblical narrative, why did your hackles rise unless what I have stated is absolutely true about people making their beliefs part of their personality? By simply reporting facts that may go against the perception of the Christian ideology, why do you feel offended as if I am attacking you personally, unless what I have shared about people embracing their beliefs as part of their personality is true? By embracing any belief, the belief becomes part of us, and to challenge the belief amounts to attacking us personally. We must defend the belief to defend ourselves.

Compassion and humanitarianism became concepts to strive for but were rarely attained. They produced a model, a mental construct, for the believers to try and achieve, but they were in conflict against what was often the basest of human nature. Although we humans have a compassionate streak in us when it is warranted, compassion and humanitarianism are failed doctrines when one has to force themselves into the unattainable false perception of either principle. The Christly concept of compassion and humanitarianism are forced concepts, unattainable by we lowly human beings, but after almost 2,000 years of Christian indoctrination in the western world, we have become convinced that these principles lie inherent in our emotional composition. Sadly, in the modern era, compassion and humanitarianism have been turned into political tools of psychological manipulation. If you are not considered *compassionate* enough to embrace fraudulent Marxist ideas cloaked in the guilt of not being humanitarian, then you are considered a callous individual and most likely a Nazi. This is how the concepts of compassion and humanitarianism have been turned into emotional weapons for cultural brainwashing at the hands of the Fabian Marxists.

Revealing what I just have is liable to spark some very negative emotional responses in some readers thinking I am attacking Christianity, but the subject matter is how the emotions of compassion and humanitarianism have been over-amplified since Buddha originally proposed the doctrine of compassion into a very violent ancient world as a possible solution for humanity to advance itself. It also illustrates how the same doctrine was embraced by tyrants in the form of the Roman emperors to quell a potentially rebellious population by shaping it into a religious ideology. In the case of Buddha, compassion was seen as a possible solution to a very violent humanity. In the case of the Pauline doctrine and the stories about Jesus and his compassion, the Romans turned compassion and humanitarianism into a weapon of emotional control and crowd subservience.

Now, lets take a look under *Humanitarianism* in Wikipedia and see what we can learn about humanitarianism. In part we are told:

*"Humanitarianism is an informal **ideology of practice**; it is "the doctrine that people's **duty** is to promote human welfare."*

*Humanitarianism is based on a view that all human beings deserve respect and dignity and should be treated as such. Therefore, humanitarians work towards advancing the well-being of humanity as a whole. It is the antithesis of the "us vs. them" mentality that characterizes **tribalism and ethnic nationalism**. Humanitarians abhor slavery, violation of basic and human rights, and discrimination on the basis of features such as skin colour, religion, ancestry, or place of birth. Humanitarianism drives people to save lives, alleviate suffering, and promote human dignity in the middle of man-made or natural disasters. Humanitarianism is embraced by movements and people across the political spectrum. The informal ideology can be summed up by a quote from Albert Schweitzer: "Humanitarianism consists in never sacrificing a human being to a purpose.""*

[Bold emphasis mine]

On its face this all sounds hunky dory but let's break this down and analyze how humanitarianism is defined. Under this definition, humanitarianism is not a choice of the individual, but is demanded as a *duty* that we must all embrace to *promote human welfare*. Who is it that defines this *duty* in the first place, and what is defined as *human welfare* in the second? Who has set themselves up as the determining authority to institute such a *duty*? Duty indicates compelled performance, an *obligation*, not an action of our own choosing. When we are told that humanitarianism is a duty, we are placed into a position of feeling guilty if we do not perform the duty of being a humanitarian. I trust you are starting to see through the charade of emotional manipulation by making humanitarianism an expected duty with the guilt associated by not bending your knee to dictated humanitarian causes. It is a guilt mechanism that is highly emphasized in the Marxist ideology to push forward their agenda of Globalist Communism. Humanitarianism in this context is turned into an emotional *weapon* to be used against humanity. If one does not meet their standards of humanitarianism, they are considered inhuman.

Globalism, in earlier decades, was referred to as the Communist International. Internationalism is in direct opposition to Nationalism. I ask you to take note of the sentence, *"It (humanitarianism)is the antithesis of the "us vs. them" mentality that characterizes **tribalism and ethnic nationalism**."* Nationalism is the sworn enemy of the Globalist Communists, the Communist International. As should be patently obvious by this one sentence alone, the concept of humanitarianism is the dutiful ideology of Globalist Communists and it is established to fight 'tribalism and ethnic nationalism'. There is no other conclusion that can be reached by such a statement. Nationalism is anti-humanitarian by its very nature in the Marxist Internationalist ideology. When you can understand this subversive ideology, then you can comprehend why the Communist Left in America is calling President Trump a Nazi for promoting his Make America Great Again program. He is a nationalist with the interests of his country at heart. According to the definition of humanitarianism above, then he must also be a racist, endorse slavery, violate human rights and everything else that comes with this Communist diatribe about the duty of humanitarianism that the Mockingbird media spews out every hour of every day since Trump got elected. Can you see the psychological and emotional game being played here yet? Is this really humanitarianism by choice, or is it a false ideology to lure the ignorant people into bolstering the Communist ideology through faux humanitarianism and political posturing?

Humanitarianism of this nature was the centerpiece of the Theosophical Society. If you read the link below produced by the Theosophical Society, you will discover exactly the same tenets voiced by Madame Helena Blavatsky in her 1889 work, *The Keys to Theosophy*. The link below points to an article entitled, *Theosophy on War and Peace* published in *Quest* magazine in 2003 by Robert S. Ellwood.

https://www.theosophical.org/publications/1606

Blavatsky's reference to "national selfishness" in the article denotes her patently Marxist leanings embedded in the alleged 'spiritual' teachings of Theosophy. It is simply the

Communist International in disguise masquerading as Theosophical spirituality.

We explained in our book, *Revamping Psychology: A Critique of Transpersonal Psychology*, how the field of Transpersonal Psychology was the brainchild of Theosophically-oriented psychologists like Stanislav Grof, as just one example. Transpersonal Psychology is incestuously connected to the sex, drugs and rock & roll culture of the 1960s and found its birthplace in Big Sur, California at Esalen Institute. It is a commonly accepted fact that the New Age Movement was born at Esalen Institute and turned into the worldwide spiritualist movement it is today, based primarily on Theosophical principles.

Along with the blending of Eastern and Western religious ideas, preaching enlightenment through advocating the use of hallucinogenic drugs promoted through such Fabian Communist fellow-travelers like Aldous Huxley, and pushing a form of false spirituality, the Theosophical Society spread its area of control through many alleged humanitarian organizations like World Goodwill, which conveniently falls under the umbrella of the Lucis Trust organization.

For those who may have never heard of Lucis Trust, this brief synopsis from Wikipedia should provide at least a foundational understanding of the organization.

"The Lucis Trust is a nonprofit service organization incorporated in the United States in 1922 by Alice Bailey and her husband Foster Bailey, to act as a fiduciary trust for the publishing

of twenty-four books of esoteric philosophy published under Alice Bailey's name, and to fund and administer activities concerned with the establishment of "right human relations". These include the Arcane School, a school for esoteric training, World Goodwill, Triangles, a lending library, The Beacon magazine, as well as the publishing company.

*The objectives of the Lucis Trust as stated in its charter are: "To encourage the study of comparative religion, philosophy, science and art; to encourage every line of thought tending to the broadening of human sympathies and interests, and the expansion of ethical religious and educational literature; to assist or to engage in activities for the relief of suffering and for human betterment; and, in general, **to further worthy efforts for humanitarian and educational ends."***

The Lucis Trust's publishing company was founded in the early 1920s as the Lucifer Publishing Company. The Lucis Trust says that the name was probably chosen to honor Lucifer. The name was changed in 1925 to the Lucis Publishing Company. In Latin lucem ferre *means "to bear light" and* lucis *means of light. The company has*

Although not a founding member, Alice Bailey was one of the early members of the British Fabian Society. Like her Communist counterpart, Annie Besant (who was a co-founder of the Fabian Society), Bailey eventually took control of Blavatsky's Theosophical Society becoming its president in the U.S., while Annie Besant took over the Eastern branch of the Society in India. As can be seen by the brief description above, the Lucis Trust organization is steeped in alleged humanitarianism principles teaching a form of spiritual docility through the organization's 30,760 subdivisions worldwide. One of these associated charitable trusts is the United Nations.

Through pushing a Fabian Marxist version of humanitarianism through its fraudulent spiritual doctrines, the Theosophical Society serves as a hidden agent to the worldwide Communist Fabian agenda. It's doctrines teach peace, love and docility, effectively brainwashing its followers into being compliant left-leaning activists and ignorantly pushing the Fabian Communist agenda mistakenly thinking they are being more 'spiritual' and Earth oriented 'Gaians'. Through these alleged spiritual doctrines, the Fabian Globalists push their bogus 'green' agenda as just one more method to deprive people of their property through Marxist-created environmental laws and other presumed compassionate humanitarian causes. I doubt very seriously that you will find many New Agers voting Republican.

It should be patently obvious after reading this chapter how people are manipulated on the emotional level with forced faux compassion and humanitarianism to fulfill the Marxist Globalist agenda. In the U.S. today, as well as in Europe, nation states are being undermined by invading hordes of alleged 'refugees' flooding into the countries of the West to ultimately undermine their independent nationhood and turn the world into a Communist international Globalist hegemony. The Communists are experts in psychological manipulation and playing on your emotional heartstrings is fair game in their quest for world domination. Hiding behind the mask of faux spirituality peddled by the Theosophical Society and Lucis Trust into the New Age Movement, as well as creeping into Christian Churches in the U.S., has been one of the most hateful subversive tactics used by these would-be Communist world rulers to control the minds of the unsuspecting compassionate masses and turn them into rabid political activists. Maybe now you are armed with enough facts to argue against 'duty' humanitarianism and see through the fraud of humanitarian compassion. It is a *weapon*, not a virtue.

6. Who Dictates Morality?

The objective of this chapter is not to dictate what anyone's particular moral views should be, but how morality is used as but one more weapon to stir emotions to control the masses. You may find that some questions I raise in this chapter will create emotional reactions in yourself as you read them. If you experience any of these emotional reactions, then you should view them as absolute proof how your emotions manipulate your thinking processes.

The first thing I will establish is that morality is purely subjective. The morals in one country may not be the morals in another country, and they will even vary within the borders of separate nations. Morality serves as a major catalyst for emotional manipulation for those who desire to control your consciousness as well as your actions. This control through morality goes back thousands of years, so it is not a new invention. Cultures and religions have used morality laws for leverage over their populations for virtually all of recorded human history. One of the earliest recorded examples of these types of laws is found in the Code of Hammurabi dated from about 1754 BC. One of the passages from these laws can be found on Wikipedia under *Code of Hammurabi*:

*"Anu and Bel called by name me,
Hammurabi, the exalted prince, who feared God,
to bring about the rule of righteousness in the land,
to destroy the wicked and the evil-doers; so that
the strong should not harm the weak; so that I
should rule over the black-headed people like
Shamash, and enlighten the land, to further the
well-being of mankind."*

As this Wikipedia reference states elsewhere:

*"Nearly half of the code deals with matters
of contract, establishing the wages to be paid to an
ox driver or a surgeon for example. Other
provisions set the terms of a transaction, the
liability of a builder for a house that collapses, or
property that is damaged while left in the care of
another. A third of the code addresses issues
concerning household and family relationships
such as inheritance, divorce, paternity, and
reproductive behaviour."*

As you can tell, Hammurabi was quite extensive in his
reach as king into the affairs of his subjects, and as the third part
of the quoted passage points out, he didn't hesitate to meddle in
household affairs, which is dictating acceptable morality for his
subjects according to his laws. Hammurabi's laws are found in
other surrounding cultures over the passing centuries, including

the Mosaic laws found in the Old Testament. The idea that the Ten Commandments were handed down by God must be questioned in light of the fact that the Code of Hammurabi predates the Hebrew exile in Egypt by many centuries. There is too much scholarly agreement that Hammurabi's Code was the predecessor of the Mosaic laws to be wholly ignored. Be that as it may, regardless of what one chooses to believe, Hammurabi's Code clearly illustrates that governments throughout time have dictated morality. This goes back to tribal laws and is reflected in later kingly or priestly laws such as Hammurabi's as well as the biblical Ten Commandments.

It doesn't really matter the source of these morality laws, they have haunted humanity throughout the ages and the cry for justice against violations of morality is only an emotional breath away from exploding in any given population depending on the morality laws of the culture, the era and what moral outrage it generates in the public mind. As such, morality laws have ever been used as weapons by cultural authorities and religious believers throughout the world over the ages. Although the numbers have been questionably fabricated by the neo-Pagans, the witch trials and witch burnings in both Europe, and the Salem witch trials, clearly illustrate what happens when emotions and fear can be put into motion over moral outrage. We saw the same fervor with the Spanish Inquisition spearheaded by Tomás de Torquemada and the demand for adherence to the Catholic faith as a moral obligation to the Church.

Two centuries prior to the Spanish Inquisition the Roman Church waged a 20-year military campaign to eradicate a form of

Gnosticism that was gathering many adherents in the Cathar breakaway religious movement. These were called the Albigensians, located in the region of Languedoc, France. The Gnostic ideology is one of those grafted into the doctrine of Theosophy and elements of Gnostic teaching can also be found in some of the four Gospels in the Bible. The Albigensian Crusade is used by the Theosophists and the New Agers as one of the most murderous acts of the Roman Church. It was a battle of religious interpretation that put the Cathars at odds with the Roman Church. To understand better you can look up *Albigensian Crusade* on Wikipedia. As Wikipedia reports about the Massacre of Béziers:

"The Crusaders captured the small village of Servian and then headed for Béziers, arriving on July 21, 1209. Under the command of the papal legate, Arnaud Amalric, they started to besiege the city, calling on the Catholics within to come out, and demanding that the Cathars surrender. Neither group did as commanded. The city fell the following day when an abortive sortie was pursued back through the open gates. The entire population was slaughtered and the city burned to the ground. It was reported that Amalric, when asked how to distinguish Cathars from Catholics, responded, "Kill them all! God will know his own." Whether this was actually said is sometimes considered doubtful, but, according to historian Joseph Strayer, it captures the "spirit" of the Crusaders,

who killed nearly every man, woman, and child in the town.

Amalric and Milo, a fellow legate, in a letter to the Pope, claimed that the Crusaders "put to the sword almost 20,000 people". Strayer insists that this estimate is too high, but noted that in his letter "the legate expressed no regret about the massacre, not even a word of condolence for the clergy of the cathedral who were killed in front of their own altar". News of the disaster quickly spread and afterwards many settlements surrendered without a fight."

Before it was all said and done, the Roman Church committed a genocide on all the Cathar heretics. Part of the Church's propaganda to disparage this opposing doctrine was to accuse the heretics of buggery (sodomy), and so morality, whether the claims were true or not, served as a catalyst for the other Crusaders to murder them wholesale. The Church revulsion of homosexuality served as enough of a catalyst to get the outraged 'straight' Crusaders to kill them all - man, woman and child.

Homosexuality has been part of the human tapestry throughout recorded history and before. In some cultures, it has been embraced as a natural part of life like in ancient Athens, and even in Rome under its stringent patriarchal system, it was allowed, so long as the man didn't take the submissive position of being penetrated. It is not the focus of this book to take a stance in any of this and dictate morality or what my own views are on the subject. The focus is to illustrate how morality serves as just another mode of emotional manipulation that the controllers of the human herds use to control those herds. Based on one single verse in the book of Leviticus in the Bible, the Christian hatred of all things homosexual will spark an emotional revulsion and has on more than one occasion led to terrible crimes.

The current political climate in the West, with the rise of transgenderism and thousands of non-binary-gender-oriented people, is also heavily fueled by emotion and hatred on both sides. As much as many Christians do not have direct responsibility for almost two thousand years of sexual repression, what we are seeing today in the political arena with people who genuinely believe that there are in fact 63 separate gender identifiers, in contradiction to scientific biological designation of only two genders, (or perhaps three if one takes into account the small number of hermaphrodites, people born with both sets of sexual organs), the modern sexual revolution is a backlash against 1,700 years of religious Christian and Muslim sexual repression and prejudice.

Contrary to what those unfamiliar with history may believe, the concept of free love did not originate with the 1960s sexual revolution. That was just the latest permutation of a doctrinal concept that goes as far back as the 6th century AD. Free love was intimately coupled with the foundations of the Feminist Movement, and after Karl Marx wrote his books, by 1857 Feminism and the free love concepts had been grafted wholesale onto Marxist socialist ideologies to challenge the moral strictures of Christianity. This war over sexuality and morals is timeless indeed, and there is no quick end in sight, particularly so long as it continues to be used as a political weapon by both sides to push their own herd agendas on other human herds through moral dictates and political agendas.

Different cultures worldwide have different morality mandates, and contrary to what some people may believe, these cultural moral dictates do not often agree. Because of generations of sexual psychological programming as well as resistance to that programming, sex and sexuality will be a hot-button moral issue for some time to come. Any demagogue can preach from a pulpit or a soapbox to spark moral outrage in people to pit them against one another, and it has been done throughout the ages. Morality and moral judgments in all their permutations have stirred the emotional pot of contention for thousands of years, and sex and sexual preferences have led the way throughout the millennia. Morality, any perceptions of morality, not just sexuality, has become a matter of herd consensus and not personal judgment or choice. To go against the herd consensus is to become immoral, even 'evil'. Welcome to the political circus in USA in the 21st century.

Those who have and would continue to control human consciousness must first manipulate one's emotions. Because one's sexuality or sexual preference is such an intimate affair and subjective in perspective, dictating herd moral codes is just another tool for psychological manipulation on an emotional level. It has worked throughout the ages and it continues to work as an emotional weapon in our cultures today.

Within the current political arena in the United States, morality has now been tied into building a barrier across our southern border with Mexico by the Marxist-leaning Democrats in the U.S. House of Representatives. "The Wall" has been turned into another aspect of the so-called moral war fabricated by the Marxist Left, and the believers in this moral myth are highly charged on an emotional level and it will only take the right spark to incite this emotional volatility into violence.

The emotional tableau in the U.S. today is little different than the emotional volatility that was present in the years leading up to the Civil War. Although the issue in the mid-19th century was about abolition of slavery, the modern equivalent is a fabricated emotional moral indignation against building a wall to insure the safety of all American citizens against an invasion of literally millions of migrant refugees. To the mind of a revolutionary Marxist, it is just one more emotional weapon to be used against a target nation slated for destruction and devolution into the Communist quagmire of tyranny and cultural destruction by calling this barrier 'immoral'.

The Fabian Society and their collaborators in the SPR were at ground zero for the launching point of Psychology. Every type of experimentation possible has been used against human test subjects, with or without their knowledge, to perfect the systems of psychological control. It is well known that in order to control the crowds that one only needs to instigate an emotional outrage over some presumed moral indignation. The Marxists claim to take the presumed moral high ground as noted in the last chapter on humanitarianism and compassion to turn their emotionally controlled herds into psychologically manipulated weapons. To destroy a nation from within, Fabian Marxists play both ends of the spectrum against each other using emotional manipulation to rile both sides in any conflict through emotionally charged propaganda. Those who are most easily swayed by their emotions, rather than rational thinking or logic, will be the ones most easily inflamed by such propaganda. This divide and conquer agenda has worked effectively to keep humanity from uniting against the tyrants throughout recorded history

One of the most volatile hot-button issues between the Left and the Right in the U.S. today is that of abortion. Most readers are probably unaware that the issues of abortion and methods of birth control have been a bone of contention for thousands of years. These are not new issues, but timeless emotional moral issues that can be traced back to ancient Greece and Rome, although they are highly amplified in our modern world of speedier communications and the ability to galvanize people from both sides of the issue into mob protests. The moral fight over abortion is ancient indeed, and it didn't start with *Roe v. Wade*. The fight over abortion is a very polarized black and white issue with no middle ground being discussed by cither side just as much today as in eras gone by. Until this issue can be discussed by cooler heads in an attempt to find some middle ground it will remain the contentious moral issue it has for millennia.

It doesn't matter whether moral indignation is spawned by a fire and brimstone preacher excoriating his congregation about their sins and the penalties of eternal damnation, or whether it is a Marxist double-talking about worker's rights and forming unions, often through violent public acts, it is the emotions that are played upon to create herds and to keep them in check once created. It matters not who preaches their brand of morality, its only through stirring the emotions toward moral indignation and outrage that presumed morality of any kind is used to homogenize herd thinking and collectivist solidarity based on these moral strictures.

When one combines moral indignation of any flavor with the mask of humanitarianism and compassion, we find a recipe for disaster where creating mobs and violence are concerned. It has worked throughout history and it is still at play today. One only need look at the world around us to see all the evidence necessary where emotions rule the mobs more than any pause for rational thought and analysis. Humanity has learned nothing throughout the ages, and psychological and emotional manipulation since the invention of the field of Psychology has only increased to become a weapon of warfare. Will humanity learn now, or will it remain as destructive as it always has been based on being ruled by its emotions rather that its reason where its alleged 'moral judgments' are concerned?

7. Thinking versus Feeling

I have developed a process in my books *Demystifying the Mystical* and *Navigating into the Second Cognition*, along with our collaborative book *The Second Cognition Toolbox* whereby a dedicated individual can remove many of the trigger programs that make our species so emotionally volatile. For the most part, we are thinking creatures, but each of us is a walking minefield of reactive emotions just waiting to be triggered when the right words are uttered to us or when a certain situation triggers our emotions into action. Once triggered the usual thinking process is immediately suspended and our emotional outburst takes the driver's seat. This fact alone should prove to every reader that we feel and react emotionally, before we think.

An emotional trigger can override all rational thought in an instant, and there is not one human being on this planet that has escaped such outbursts probably many times during their lives. How many times have you exploded over some sense of being offended to return later to the person you dumped your vitriol on and apologize by saying you didn't know what came over you? If you have ever done this, or seen someone else do it, then it should be patently obvious that emotional triggers take priority over any thinking processes to the contrary. However, thinking processes can be coupled with emotional senses of being offended where one can stew for hours over some perceived sleight, work their anger up, then dump their emotional garbage at the doorstep of the person who offended them. But even in these cases where the thinking mind comes into the picture to plot and plan how to redress the perceived wrong, it is still an emotional trigger that preceded the mental process of stewing over the offense. Something sparked the emotion before the thinking and stewing process began. In cases like this, the thinking process and the emotional process turn into a self-feeding loop until the emotional release finally alleviates and breaks the loop.

The reason we have these emotional reactions is that we all have something to protect, and that is our self-image, what is commonly known as the ego. When we trigger emotionally on whatever sets us off, it is because the ego part of our psyche feels threatened when a part of its own self-image is challenged. This challenge can be against us on a personal basis in the form of a personal insult, and it can be equally triggered when we find our beliefs challenged, for the ego adopts its beliefs as part of its personal identity. To challenge one's beliefs amounts to an assault on the individual, particularly if it is a very closely held belief like a religious belief or political ideology. We also develop emotional defensive mechanisms in many cases in favor of our sports teams and will rise to actual fist fights if someone from the other team says your team sucks and it hits you wrong depending on how loyal you are to your team.

If we find ourselves in a group setting and the insults or attacks are deemed serious enough, mob violence can, and often does break out, sometimes even leading to large scale warfare.

Assault and insult someone's honor or national pride and the national mob will band together to go get the offender with little questioning. Once the emotional spark of national outrage is ignited, then warfare is soon to follow. History has proven this time and again.

To inspire a nation to go to war with another only requires sparking the sense of emotional moral outrage and the desire for revenge, and nations will rush off to kill their adversaries. Once these emotions are put into motion with skillfully planted propaganda to beat the war drums, the emotions escalate and the fervor for revenge stays hot in the public mob mind. Once these emotions are sparked, the only thinking process that results from this public emotional inflaming is planning on how many of the enemy we can kill and the battle lust kicks in, which is simply more emotional strengthening. Again, history provides all the evidence necessary to verify this. I cite the false flag incidents of the sinking of the Lusitania, the contrived attacks on Pearl Harbor and the totally fictional Gulf of Tonkin incident which was the foundation of starting the Vietnam war. To these calculated events we can add the 9/11 attacks as one more example that led to the last 17 years of warfare in the Middle East.

A contrived act like a false flag is all that is necessary to galvanize a country into going to war. Hitler was able to rise to power because of an economic depression that made the German Mark virtually worthless, and continued violence by communist agitators like Antifa who were mostly spearheaded by Jewish Marxists. Sanitized Western history would have us all believe that Hitler just hated Jews for no cause and so he targeted them for no reason in his rise to power, merely using them as a scapegoat to galvanize the German people to get behind him with his Aryan racial superiority doctrine. The West is not told of the legitimate and actual hard communist Jewish influence in the streets as well as in academia, just like we see the same thing happening in America today (minus the specifically Jewish element). Nothing happens in a vacuum, and the political climate in the U.S. today is little different than what occurred in Germany with the communists seeking to undermine and take over the German government in the 1930s. The tactics are the same, the methods are the same, and with Antifa, the communist organizations are the same as they were just less than 100 years ago. Marxism is being indoctrinated in our schools in America today just as it was being promoted by Jewish communist activists in Germany in the 1930s. The perpetrators may vary racially, but the communist ideology has not changed one iota.

Because Western history has been sanitized of these facts by Fabian Marxist publishing houses that control educational publishing, Americans are clueless of the gradualist subversion of the Fabian Marxists and the psychological war waged against the American public for more than a century. With at least 95% of our media outlets in print and TV serving as collaborators to this Marxist Globalist agenda, the public is not informed of the facts and can only swim in a sea of emotional confusion, seeking answers to what is wrong with America and no longer having a trusted media to provide them with the facts.

Americans have been deliberately and maliciously dumbed-down to the level of uninformed cattle to the communist agenda, spending more time seeking sensationalist stories about meaningless Hollywood elite and their pro-communist talking points, or brain-draining hours a day in front of a TV watching escapist presentations that have little to do with educating them. The public demands what will excite its emotions, not what will advance its consciousness and make them more critical thinkers. From sappy romantic comedies and the alleged aches over women seeking Mr. Right to the continual onslaught of superhero movies and adventure films filled with violence, to the cop shows that do not teach anything real about the law but a thin Hollywood propaganda veneer about the law, the public has an insatiable desire for emotional gratification. In collusion with the media and Operation Mockingbird, the American people live in a political echo chamber where all they hear about is hate Trump and hate our form of government, all while socialist communists keep trying to paint us a picture of their utopian world of destruction. Venezuela is a shining example of the communist utopia in full bloom.

Socialism has always thrived in an environment of emotional control, and do not lose sight of the fact that Hitler was a Socialist. He only peddled a brand of National Socialism in conflict with the International Communism driven by the Jewish commissars. The American political climate today is little different than Hitler's Germany where riling the public's emotions comes into play. It was the same in every communist revolution from the Paris commune in the mid-1800s, through the Bolshevik Revolution to Castro and every other socialist-turned-dictator throughout history. Communism can only take hold when it can convince people on an emotional level that they are victims of one sort or another. Once you have identified yourself as part of a victim class, you are emotionally ripe for the picking of communist agitators. The mind of a critical thinker can see through this charade, but few can rise above the emotional manipulation to think critically enough to expose the charade to themselves. They are too interested in seeking emotional feel-good escapism or too busy being an offended victim to think for themselves. Either way, cognitive laziness leaves the public prey to this kind of emotional manipulation and mind control techniques.

People with wisdom are worried about psychological warfare, but the fact is that the road to controlling the psyche runs through the emotions first. In my book, *The Psychology of Becoming Human: Evolving Beyond Psychological Conditioning,* I provided overwhelming evidence that proves beyond the shadow of a doubt that since the inception of the field of psychology, it has been used as a weapon against the public. Whether the psychological warfare waged against the public is through 'public relations' and marketing consumer goods, to controlling the public's perceptions on politics and religion, psychology has been the weapon of choice of the Fabian Marxists to wage war against the American way of life. Before anyone can get 'brainwashed', their emotions have to be hooked first, for the emotions lead to the psyche.

It is not widely known to the public at large yet, although other researchers have discovered what I have in regard to certain inventions by Hendricus G. Loos. Loos is a rather enigmatic person about whom you can find little background information except his operating in the field of aviation for many years. Beyond this information, finding any information about Loos is a void. The link below will take you to a list of U.S. Patents granted to Hendricus Loos going back to 1978 at *Justia Patents*. I ask you to look up this website and familiarize yourself with these patents so you can keep up with the explanations in the subsequent chapters.

https://patents.justia.com/inventor/hendricus-g-loos

The patents that will be discussed in the following pages will be those since 1992 and, as you will note, most of them have to do with devices that manipulate the human nervous system through microvolt signals transmitted through computer terminals and televisions. Even the researchers who I have looked into who found the Loos patents have not discovered the full impact of the Loos devices on human physiology, but they have been wise enough to suspect a dastardly intent behind their invention and application. The next few chapters are going to reveal a massive horror story about manipulating human consciousness through subliminal electronic nervous system manipulation to generate false emotional triggers, and the reader's first reaction will be to deny what is going to be revealed because of the magnitude of what it portends for world culture.

Through frequency control devices like the Loos patents, stimulating the human nervous system subliminally excites emotions with everything from a desire to rush out and buy a new product to being driven by fear over dire news reports and every emotion in between. Psychological programming does not work without the element of emotional excitation to set the programming in place to eventually feed into the psyche. All the controllers need to do to engage the psyche is get their hooks into your emotions first. This aspect will be discussed at length about Loos' Patent No. 5995954 - *Method and apparatus for associative memory*, in greater detail later on.

Once the emotional hook is set, the psychological programming of the selective propaganda matrix, whether product ads, political ideologies, or religious and spiritual beliefs, the psyche follows the emotions when a contrived narrative is coupled with the subliminally generated emotional response through a form of emotional 'association'. The emotions are stimulated through the central nervous system (CNS) and those who demand to control your minds know how to control your emotions through CNS manipulation and the Loos frequencies. It is one of the most subversive and dastardly agendas imaginable and people worldwide have been subjected to such frequencies manipulating their emotional states in order to control their minds for decades.

Although you may read the patents for the Loos' inventions, they are going to come across to most people as incomprehensible technical gibberish because the main intent for the invention of these devices is well hidden from the public in techno-speak. Although I am not going to address each specific patent, by the time the next few chapters are completed, you should have a layman's working knowledge of what these devices do and how they are abused to control most of humanity through emotional manipulation and psychological control. It is going to be a very unpleasant realization to see how our cultures have been manipulated through such a manner of hateful frequency warfare aimed at our emotions to keep us harnessed into fraudulent belief systems and create a false perception of reality. The acceptance threshold will be your own having to admit that you have been manipulated in this manner just like everyone around you has for years. That is the big red pill that most would rather deny than swallow.

8. Religion and Spirituality

Probably the oldest form of mind control traces back through all world religions to the stories of the ancient gods. Although more modern offspring of these ancient belief systems (Judaism, Christianity and Islam) claim to be somehow removed from this ancient form of crowd mind control, I think I capably proved the contrary in my large volume, *Gutting Mysticism: Explaining the Roots of All Supernatural Beliefs*. That particular volume will shock the reader in both the ideas it proposes as well as the range of research presented to make up the 500-page presentation.

What I am going to reveal in this chapter is a snapshot of data presented, not only in *Gutting Mysticism*, but throughout the 31 volumes we have written to lay the foundation to expose the real history of humanity that lies behind the illusion we perceive as our reality. I struggled mightily over whether to present the information that follows in this volume as it is primarily designed for a mainstream audience who either chooses to live in denial of these facts, or who would simply call me crazy for presenting them and discount everything in this book as fallacy. If the reader gives me the chance to explain all these things with a genuinely open mind, then you should come away with a different picture of reality than the one you presently perceive. I only ask that you give me that chance to show you how this all threads together into a comprehensive tapestry of a history that has been hidden behind the veil of tyranny since human beings on this planet were created.

In 1968 the author Erich von Daniken proposed the idea that the gods referred to in ancient literature were actual beings who came from the heavens. Although I am not particularly an aficionado of von Daniken, especially since he has been caught up in fraudulently falsifying much of his 'evidence', this is where the door opened into the public awareness of ancient aliens standing in the roles of the ancient gods. His ideas found fertile ground in the burgeoning UFO movement, particularly after the sensationalist event of an alleged crash of an alien spaceship in Roswell, New Mexico in 1947. The term flying saucer was coined as early as 1930, but the U.S. Air Force changed the term to unidentified flying object (UFO) in 1952.

To be up front with the reader, I am not a UFO nut and I am not bound by the belief that we have aliens constantly buzzing our planet for shits and giggles. My ideas may be another story for another place and time, but it goes beyond the scope of this book to get sidetracked into that particular rabbit hole. Let's just say that I don't believe in all this current alien UFO mythology and I believe there are plenty of sound explanations about UFO crafts built right here on Earth to create the elusive lights in the sky continually reported.

In 1976, the next players to enter onto the ancient aliens' stage were Zechariah Sitchin with his book *The 12th Planet*; and the book by Robert K.G. Temple entitled *The Sirius Mystery*. Of these two authors, Sitchin gained the most traction and notoriety with his stories about the ancient Sumerian gods known as the Anunnaki, since he continued to write more and more books about the alleged family feuds between these ancient offworld entities based on his own interpretations of ancient Mesopotamian texts. Sadly, Sitchin, like von Daniken, took too much liberty with the textual evidence he provided, often creating his own translations to spin his tales just as von Daniken fabricated evidence to bolster his stories. The tales of the Anunnaki, or Anunna gods, abound in ancient Mesopotamian texts and there is no shortage of textual evidence on clay tablets that tell the stories of these gods who came from heaven even in mainstream archaeological translations.

Where I am going with all this is that every religious tradition on the planet into the modern era is centered around its believers 'serving god'. Along with this mandate to serve God, we also find that there is a concept that some God or another created mankind. In my thinking, it doesn't make much difference in believing that Earth humans were created by some invisible God that created life, the universe and everything, or whether humans on this planet were created in a genetic laboratory to serve the needs of offworld entities who needed slaves to do their work and passed themselves off as our creator gods. In both cases, we are a 'created' species. So, to me, this is not a point worth quibbling over as it is only a matter of doctrinal belief and little else.

There is a secondary factor that is going to stretch the reader's credulity, and that is that humanity (including these ancient so-called gods) was infected with what you could call a cosmic mind virus, which we define in our writings as the hapiym mind virus. The word hapiym is an acronym for HAcker Program In Your Mind. I explained this mind virus in depth in my book *The Energetic War Against Humanity: The 6,000 Year War Against Human Cognitive Advancement.*

Probably the first mainstream idea of a cosmic mind virus found its way into public awareness with the writings of Carlos Castenada and the teachings of the Yaqui sorcerer he called don Juan. Don Juan referred to this mind virus as a 'predator from the stars' who preys on the energy field of all humans in order to nourish itself. Don Juan claimed that this virus achieved this 'stupendous' act by giving humanity 'its' mind.

The next person to weigh in on this type of mind virus was Jack Forbes in his book *Columbus and Other Cannibals* published in 1992. Forbes' idea was far removed from the concept that don Juan proposed about the mind virus being a predator from the stars, and his interpretation of the mind virus was that Capitalism and only Western Europeans were infected with it. Being a left-leaning Native American, Forbes had a political Marxist axe to grind with his proposed mind virus concepts, so he was very wide of the mark of reality with his conjectures about the hapiym mind virus.

The next person to address the mind virus with any seriousness was Paul Levy in his out-of-print book, *Wetiko: The Greatest Epidemic Sickness Known to Humanity* published in 2011. The original volume has since been expanded and rereleased under the title, *Dispelling Wetiko: Breaking the Curse of Evil* published in 2013. Prior to writing my own *Energetic War* book, I had heard of neither of the latter two authors.

Where Forbes used the Native American concept of a Wendigo or Wetiko as the foundation to attack Capitalism as a mental disorder imported to the Americas by European settlers to forward his own Marxist-leaning beliefs, Levy comes out of the modern spiritual school of neo-shamanism, professing to be able to cure this Wetiko mind virus with quasi-New Age spiritual techniques. To date, I haven't seen where Paul Levy's alleged shamanic techniques have gained any footage in curing the symptoms of the mind virus because he had no full concept of what this virus really was or how it operated, and lastly how to deal with the symptomatology to eradicate the residuals of the virus infection.

In all honesty, to get a more accurate perspective of the mind virus prior to my work, you would have to read a 1967 science fiction book by Colin Wilson entitled *The Mind Parasites* to get close to understanding the hapiym mind virus. Again, I did not even know about Wilson's book until someone had read my *Energetic War* book, and recommended I read it in a comment posted on our YouTube channel. Still and all, Wilson's book comes much closer to defining the control of the hapiym mind virus than either Forbes or Levy and more closely resembles the teachings of don Juan about an invading predator from the stars that 'gave us its mind' to control humanity.

This foundation, as hard as it may be to accept, is a necessary element in progressing into how religions and spirituality have been a major form of mind control throughout human history, and how emotional manipulation keeps these beliefs in place as much as any other belief we embrace. It is not my job in this book to rewrite or rehash what I have written about extensively elsewhere, but only provide a snapshot of information to prove how emotionalism rules our perceptions of reality, even our perceptions of God.

Throughout recorded history there have been seers and sages, those who could allegedly speak with the dead or prophets who could allegedly commune with God or the gods. There is no shortage of textual evidence from ancient Egypt, Greece, Rome, India, China and elsewhere where people, either with special talents, or those under the influence of psychotropic substances, could talk with their gods, angels or dead ancestors. Although modern Christians try and rationalize away that their saints and prophets were somehow different than pagan sages with similar talents, in the long run there truly is not a distinction beyond the perceptual *belief* that there is any real difference. I explain this in depth with no shortage of explanatory and textual proof in *Gutting Mysticism*.

To understand the hapiym mind virus you have to look at a beehive with a single queen and a hive mind that operates under her control. The hapiym virus was a hive mind. It replicated its 'cells' into the human form and then duplicated the personality of its human host creating a false ego, a doppelganger of the real person's personality. Then this infectious mind parasite virus cell convinced you that the infectious duplicate cell was really you. Levy at least got this much right in his *Dispelling Wetiko* book.

Upon death, the human form dies, yet this energetic virus doppelganger of the human personality lived on. One could say it was basically eternal. Through the ancient arts of necromancy and the Spiritist movements of the 17th and 18th centuries, the craze was to talk to dead ancestors to learn about life on the other side, what people presumed to be 'heaven' or 'hell'. This is no different with the modern fascination over the same topics as presented in John Edwards' TV show *Crossing Over*. Humans are and have ever been enchanted with knowing about the afterlife. This is also explained in exquisite detail in *Gutting Mysticism* and I am not going to recap it all here. In the 19th and 20th century, this practice of talking to 'spirits' wove its way into the New Age arena at the hands of the Theosophical Society and is known as channeling. Both Madame Blavatsky and Alice Bailey were channelers and much of their writing revolves around entities they referred to as the Ascended Masters. This same terminology wormed its way into the New Age vernacular.

While the hapiym virus hive was still alive and functioning (which it no longer is), most people who thought they were channeling dead relatives, aliens, angels or God, were in fact only connecting into the hapiym virus hive network and being fed false information by virus cells of their dead human hosts that substantiated their individual beliefs. They were able to connect to the hive collective consciousness through the hive cell that lived in their own body and mind through a form of sympathetic psychic resonance. If they were Christians, they were led to believe they were talking to the Saints or Angels or God; if they were of the New Age religious persuasion, it was dead relatives, Angels, Aliens or 'the Source' or 'Creator'. Through the use of psychedelic substances, the cognitive threshold of the waking human personality could be 'weakened' enough for this hive doppelganger cell inside the human host to connect with the hapiym hive virus network and take control enough of the host consciousness and fill their heads with all sorts of perceptual illusions and beliefs. The stamp of validity to all these experiences was delivered as an emotional 'rush', what Transpersonal Psychologists refer to as a 'peak experience', or what Christians or others may refer to as an epiphany. These emotional surges, manipulated by the virus itself, often led to 'instant conversions' in many cases, and the religions of the world know how to manipulate these emotional responses to set the emotional triggers for such instantaneous conversions – or finding God.

I wrote in previous chapters about the third leg of the Fabian Society-Theosophical Society triad being the Society for Psychical Research (SPR). The members of the SPR, as noted in prior chapters, had a revolving door interface with the other two organizations where the three different Society's management was concerned. They were all in it together. The 'fathers' of American and French psychology, William James and Pierre Janet, respectively, were both members of the SPR and started wings of the SPR in their respective countries. The primary purpose of the early research of the SPR was to discover human psychic abilities, and they studied medium after medium within the Spiritist movement to prove life after death and the continuance of the 'soul' by testing mediums and their capability to talk to 'spirits of the dead'. This information is not in question as it is heavily documented and easily available in books written by the members of the SPR themselves.

There were naturally many fraud artists within the Spiritist movement who would manufacture mechanical tricks in parlor seances to bilk people out of their money to talk to dead relatives, and certain members of the SPR, like the magician Harry Houdini and others, gained their notoriety by exposing fake mediums. Even though she created the Theosophical Society and may have possessed certain talents as a medium, Madame Blavatsky was eventually 'exposed' as a fraud as well (and there was evidentiary ground for her parlor chicanery to do so). But by 'exposing' Blavatsky and other mediums, the SPR distracted away from the fact that they were doing continual research into psychical studies in the background. By discrediting the Spiritist movement, it drew public attention away from what the SPR continued to research behind the scenes, and that was to figure out how to manipulate human consciousness through psychology and learning everything it could about the hapiym mind virus and how it functioned within the human body and psyche.

Sigmund Freud and Carl Jung were doing their own experimentation smoking hash and imbibing other substances while they were developing their theories of Psychology, as were many others in the field, and as many Transpersonal Psychologists in the field continue to do today, all pursuing the 'Divine' peak experience and commune with God or the cosmos. A posthumous diary of Carl Jung's visionary quests and experiences is cataloged in *The Red Book*.

It is my firm conviction, and there is no shortage of literary and doctrinal documentation to prove this, that the unholy triad of the Fabians, Theosophists and SPR worked with full knowledge of and in full collusion with the hapiym hive mind over the last century; continuing a tradition from the ancient Zoroastrianism in Persia, the Brahmin Vedic religions and goddess cults of India, the stories of the underworld and the land of the dead in ancient Mesopotamian writings, through Egypt and China, into ancient Greece and Rome, passed down through the alleged Hermetic writings of Hermes Trismegistus (Hermes the Thrice Great), into Gnosticism and into the writings of Christian composers in the New Testament Gospels; passed on through saints like Hildegard von Bingen, through the Renaissance into Rosicrucianism, into the Romance literature and philosophy of the 17th and 18th century, through the Knights Templar and the subsequent transformation into the Freemasonic societies and the Illuminati of Adam Weishaupt, to finally take root in Marxism and Fabian Globalism in the present era.

I realize what a hard, red pill this is to swallow, but it is all heavily documented in all my works seeking to reveal the truth of humanity's past, particularly the books mentioned in this volume thus far. It has taken me 30 years of study into comparative religion, psychology, metaphysics, religion and spiritual beliefs, history, law and politics to put this entire puzzle together. While the Fabian Society set its focus on controlling the political narrative, the SPR worked to develop psychology and use it as a weapon, all the while masquerading psychology to the public as a 'healing art'. The Theosophical Society and its New Age spinoffs, along with the World Council of Churches and other religions like Unitarianism and Mormonism, to name just two, served to drive the new spiritual agenda of the hapiym hive virus conquest of human consciousness. Through these three primary agencies we find control over humanity's body (politic), mind (psychology) and spirit (hive virus), and this is the hidden aspect behind all the modern spiritual hype about body, mind and spirit being fed to the public through media-promoted practices of yoga and meditation and pursuing altered states of consciousness through drug use as in Transpersonal Psychology, neo-shamanism and occultism.

This triumvirate of power had a direct hand in creating the League of Nations, which finally matured into the United Nations in the 1940s. The UN is incestuously associated with the Lucis Trust organization mentioned in prior chapters, as well as the Rockefeller Foundation, the Ford Foundation, the Carnegie Foundation and a multitude of other non-governmental agencies (NGOs) worldwide. The spirituality of the UN is the spirituality of Theosophy. The agenda of this triumvirate of power is a hybrid form of quasi-spiritualist Marxism in their quest for a New World Order.

The hapiym virus, as don Juan taught about these predators, feeds on the energies emitted by human emotions, which will be discussed in greater detail as we move forward, for you must understand how the psychological manipulation of mind control actually works to be able to free your consciousness from the cognitive slavery of the illusions you think are your reality. Through emotional and psychological manipulation, humanity has been just as don Juan described what the predator from the stars did to us – we have been kept like chickens in a coop, ruled by hidden tyrannical masters who had taken over our bodies as nothing more than an energetic food supply to keep itself alive forever. The evidence that follows in the next few chapters is going to read like a horror story if you can accept the validity of what it reveals. The purpose of this book is not to frighten but to empower the reader by becoming aware of this hidden tyranny and taking steps to free their consciousness from this vile war against human consciousness.

Before an enemy can be defeated in any war, they must be identified, and their tactics revealed before an effective counterattack and victory can be achieved. This book is designed to show you the battlefield of your own mind, who is manipulating it, and how they have been doing it to humanity for time immemorial. With the advent of our technological era, since the introduction of mass media communication starting with the radio in the early 20th century, this agenda for mind control has become more pervasive and subversive than you can imagine, especially when coupled with the abuse of psychology as a weapon to herd entire cultures into situations most wanted to avoid, like two World Wars. The following chapters will provide even more grisly details of this human horror story than you have ever found revealed anywhere in human history – at least not beyond the strictures of the secret experimental centers controlled by the human tyrants that rule this planet. We start in the next chapter by describing what human emotions are.

9. What Are Emotions?

Emotion is defined as:

- a natural instinctive state of mind deriving from one's circumstances, mood, or relationships with others.

- instinctive or intuitive feeling as distinguished from reasoning or knowledge –

Merriam Webster defines **Instinct** as

- a natural or inherent aptitude, impulse, or capacity

- a largely *inheritable and unalterable tendency of an organism to make a complex and specific response to environmental stimuli without involving reason*

- *behavior that is mediated by reactions below the conscious level*

Intuition

1 : quick and ready insight

2a *: immediate apprehension* or cognition

b : knowledge or conviction gained by intuition

c : the power or faculty of *attaining to direct knowledge or cognition without evident rational thought and inference*

Feeling is defined as:

(1) : the one of the basic physical senses of which the skin contains the chief end organs and of which the sensations of touch and temperature are characteristic : **TOUCH**

(2) : a sensation experienced through this sense

b : generalized bodily consciousness or sensation

c : appreciative or responsive awareness or recognition

(experience a feeling of safety)

2a : *an emotional state or reaction*

(a kindly feeling toward the boy)

2b **feelings** plural : *susceptibility to impression*: SENSITIVITY

(the remark hurt her feelings)

3a : *the undifferentiated background of one's awareness considered apart from any identifiable sensation, perception, or thought*

b : *the overall quality of one's awareness*

c : *conscious recognition* : SENSE

4a : often *unreasoned opinion or belief* : SENTIMENT

(What are your feelings about this subject?)

b : PRESENTIMENT

(I have a feeling she's not going to like this.)

5 : *capacity to respond emotionally especially with the higher emotions*

(found out how much feeling his mother really had)

[Italics mine]

I ask the reader to take note that all these definitions refer to emotions as an 'instinct' or 'intuitive feeling based upon no reasoning or knowledge' and that they are 'inheritable'. Also note that feeling in its primary interpretation is associated with the sense of 'touch'. I direct your attention now to the italicized portions of the definitions of feelings (plural) in regard to emotional feelings. You must be aware that these definitions fit into both the materialist scientific realm of definition as well as that of psychology. You will note in the last italicized passage a reference to the 'higher emotions', yet there is little other information to define a thing about emotions, either higher or otherwise. Emotional type feelings are at best defined as "the undifferentiated background of one's awareness considered apart from any identifiable sensation, perception, or thought". So, we have to ask what this undifferentiated background is that the definition refers to.

In light of this genuine lack of definition about what emotions *are*, or what emotional sensitivity *is*, it should be obvious to the reader that neither psychology nor science has done anything more than observe emotions as a sort of given framework where human beings are concerned, i.e. *they don't know what emotions are or why we have them and exhibit them.* The fact that virtually every human being comports themselves with emotions is simply a *given*. The fact that humans pretty much universally display the same emotions the same way is where they come up with that part of the definition about what the 'undifferentiated background' means. Don Juan once posed a rhetorical question to Carlos Castenada and asked, "Have you ever noticed that once you remove the cultural veneer, that people around the world respond to the same stimuli in the same way?" What don Juan was observing is the fact that all humans operate from the same emotional template, regardless of their race, culture or sex, everywhere on the planet. Emotions are the universal constant in human behavior no matter where you are in the world. Happy is happy, sad is sad, angry is angry, depressed is depressed, etc. all across the emotional spectrum. In light of this fact, why have science and psychology taken this as a *given* without delving into the *why* of this emotional constant? The answer to this question lies in the fact that science is focused strictly on material reality, cataloging only what can be seen and measured. This is why we are told we have only 5 primary senses associated strictly with the physical/material parts of our body. Emotions are not physical. They can't be measured with eyes, tongues, noses, ears or skin, so emotions, because there is no associative material organ through which to interpret emotions, is not considered one of the primary sensing mechanisms of the human form. Yet every human is wired with the same 'equipment' with their emotions, just as we generally possess the other five sense organs in common. The fact that science has overlooked emotions as another form of sensory array possessed by humans and animals to navigate their world environment is rather staggering if you think about it.

What I am about to propose I have not seen reported anywhere else. This doesn't mean that someone has not reached the conclusions I am about to share, only that I am unaware of any source, scholarly or otherwise, that has proposed what you are about to read. It appears that no matter where you look, whether in science, psychology or spirituality, everyone just accepts that we have emotions as a 'given' without question. But the question begs asking, why are emotions and emotional responses generally standard and homogenous across the human spectrum? What makes everyone react with the same emotional reactions when faced with the correct stimulus to make them smile or cry? It seems that no one has queried *why* we have emotions at all. I am about to give you the why.

Through the rise of technology, the HeartMath Institute has been doing research into the human bio-magnetic or bioelectric field and doing some research into how emotions can affect people in a similar manner when this bio-magnetic or bioelectric field interacts with someone else's bioelectric field of energy. HeartMath's research has measured something similar to an invisible 'bubble' of subtle bio-energy that surrounds every human being, and that emotions are what are active within this field. They have also discovered that this invisible bubble can extend as far as 12 feet outside the person's body. I am not going to reanalyze the work that the HeartMath Institute has done in their research and will direct the reader to their website for further personal investigation.

https://www.heartmath.com/institute-of-heartmath/

Although HeartMath Institute has been primarily focused on this energy field being centered in the heart; and given that it has sort of a spiritual focus and is primarily looking into how to get everyone to deal from a center of love, *a la* New Age thinking, it doesn't discount what they have discovered about this bioelectric bubble that surrounds every human being in one degree or another (how far their individual field bubble reaches). I am not sold on the idea that this expanded bioelectric field originates or is governed strictly by the heart as HeartMath has concluded. Since the Institute's focus is rather spiritually oriented in the love and light doctrine, and they are interested in where the 'love energy' is triggered in the human form, then their focus would naturally be drawn to the heart where their assumptions and conclusions are concerned.

What I will suggest is that our emotions are a form of 6th or 7th sense (since ESP has already been labeled as the 6th sense). I will assert that our emotions are another standard sensory manifestation of the human form just like our other 5 primary senses, to help us navigate our way through life. The human emotional template is the same in just about everyone, barring psychopaths and those whose emotional centers do not function normally based on having experienced traumas of one kind or another in their lives. Whereas the other 5 senses have organs associated with them, the emotional sensory array is more bio-magnetic or bioelectric where our whole body is in fact the sense organ that translates data from the atmosphere around us through this extended bio-electric bubble that the HeartMath Institute has discovered and measured in their research.

I realize that this is a new concept to wrap your head around, but without taking this into consideration, what follows in the subsequent chapters will not make a lot of sense where manipulating humanity is concerned.

The human emotional sensory network runs through the entire nervous system. Our nervous system and neural network run throughout the human body. According to scientific measurement and speculation, the human body has 95-100 billion neurons or nerve cells. This neural network is what I suggest comprises the 6th sense of the emotional sensory array. I am going to stay with 6th sense in defining the emotional sensing capability within this context because it is a universal standard, whereas ESP is not universal. It takes little effort to look up on Google articles and papers on human bioelectricity or bio-magnetics as a scientific given. This is not some fringe concept.

Where mainstream science has failed to make the leap of logic to couple the nervous system with emotions mystifies me, but we also have to remember that science as we know it is still in its infancy with only about 300 years of materialist scientific experimentation to move us into the age of technology in which we presently live. It wasn't until 1822 that Louis Pasteur discovered microbes and germs when he built the first microscope to prove their existence, rather than the common belief that illnesses were caused by bad 'vapors'.

By stating that mainstream science has not reported this widely to the public, there are other aspects of science that are kept off the public radar, such as the Loos technologies mentioned in the last chapter, and these devices will be of keen import as we move forward. The fact is that certain schools of science have figured out that you can manipulate human emotions by tampering with the nervous system through electronic or magnetic signals as I will discuss in more depth later. For the present, let's stay on point in explaining how the nervous system is the sensory organ that determines emotions.

Each emotion, as discovered by HeartMath, operates from a certain frequency, sort of like a radio dial. As a simplistic example, the radio station that triggers the love emotion is a different station than the one that delivers the anger emotion, or the other range of emotions. It is all frequency generated, much like a radio for simple comparative purposes. Let's take laughter as an example. I'm sure you know someone who has that contagious type of laughter, and when they get to laughing, you can't help but join in the laughter with them. There is a frequency for this laughter. The reason you get caught up in this person's laughter is because they are strongly emitting the laughter into their bioelectric field. Being in close proximity, your bioelectric field bubble interacts with their bubble and you come into a form of energetic frequency entrainment and you laugh too. You may not have heard the joke or what caused the laughter, but because of the strength of their field, your body responds through this field interaction, triggering your nervous system and neurons and you find yourself laughing along with them but not knowing why on a conscious thinking level. This example is provided to illustrate how the emotional nervous system reacts to external field stimuli whether the brain knows why or not. You could perhaps call this instinctive, but if so, why is it considered only an instinct? What makes your body respond to their laughter when you may not even know the joke? And in such a case, do you really have any power to stop your body from reacting in a similar manner in the face of such a powerful energetic stimulus? This reaction is founded in what we refer to as the *bodymind.*

Contrary to science's lack of defining the human body as a full-scale energetic sensing organ, it has chosen to break sensing down into the strictly material realm of measurement and the 5 primary sense organs. It has not generally considered the entire body as a sensing organ in its own right. The fact of the matter is that emotions are not mental or psychological, they are *physiological* in origin. Emotions trigger in advance of any thinking or psychological processes, which indicates that something other than psychological thinking processes can trigger an emotional reaction faster than the mind is even aware of. When someone hits you the wrong way, your emotions trigger without a thought. You react *physiologically* to whatever stimulus set you off without a thought. This is the neural system of the bodymind reacting in a fight or flight mode before the signal ever reaches the brain. The best example of this I can give is, how many times have you blown up emotionally on someone, or seen someone else do it, and then come back later to apologize and say, "I don't know what came over me", as I presented previously? The fact is that the neural network of the bodymind responds to emotional stimulus faster than the brain kicks into gear to analyze what triggers the *physiological* emotional reaction.

In the modern political spectrum, particularly with the emotionally volatile leftists, the word 'trigger' has become a standard part of the vernacular. Each of us has different triggers, elements that trigger an emotional response without any thought required. We are each a walking minefield, emotionally speaking, and most of us are totally unaware of what we may see, have said to us, or done to us that will trigger an adverse emotional reaction.

These triggers are buried deep in our cellular memory and link to the neural network of the central nervous system as part of the bodymind's sensory array as our 6th sense.

Every living creature on this planet is programmed at the foundational level with the fight or flight programming. It is a survival mechanism found in every species. It is this core programming for survival that drives all our actions at its root. Beyond physical fight or flight, kill or be killed, we are also programmed on a higher scale of this survival ladder to protect ourselves on the emotional as well as on the psychological level. Whenever we feel threatened, insulted, have our beliefs challenged or whatever, we react emotionally to the information, and equally so to the messenger who delivers the unpleasant news that we do not want to hear or accept. When you can understand the fight or flight mechanism to include not only physical survival, but also psychological and emotional survival, then you start to understand human emotional reactivity. When you hear people after verbal arguments, how often have you heard, "Well I was only defending myself"? This one statement alone illustrates that we have just as much an investment in protecting ourselves emotionally, as much as we do physically. Psychology has figured out this part of emotional reactivity, but they do not know how to cure the problem. Psychologists just accept the emotions gauged by the template of the human norm which is naturally predicated on cultural standards of 'acceptable' human behavior which they have only 'observed'.

In many cases emotions are triggered by outside stimulus, but the fact is that reminiscing a fond or a bad memory can also trigger an emotional response physiologically when we revisit certain incidents. The emotional reaction may not be as strong as the original incident, but the memory of the emotion is embedded in our cellular memory for recall if the necessity ever comes up. The human body is a recording device, a tape recorder of all our life experiences. The 5 primary senses as well as the emotional 6th sense comprise this memory unit which ultimately processes through the brain as the interpretive circuit for all the other sensory input. To illustrate the point that the bodymind is the memory unit, any one of these 6 senses can trigger a memory. For instance, when I get that certain smell of fall in the air, it triggers memories of state fairs and Halloween. I don't have to think about this, just the smell in the air alone triggers the memory. We can each have similar memory triggers from the other five senses as well as what memories may spring up from a similar emotional sensory trigger. The body remembers whether the brain does or not. The most classic example I can give is with PTSD. When someone goes through major traumatic episodes, they often bury the memories in their mind, but all it takes is a trigger from another stimulus to bring the memory flooding back to us. In cases of military PTSD, the sound of a car backfiring can send someone to the pavement thinking they are under fire in a war zone based on such a triggered memory response from an auditory noise.

We all carry hidden memory triggers from our lives. To the best of my knowledge, no one has lived a perfect, pristine life without some teasing, getting beat up on the school yard, being embarrassed in one situation or another, or having a car accident. This is particularly true where virtually every culture around the planet uses shame or guilt as methods of cultural programming and reinforcement of cultural norms. Because of this cultural programming, coupled with our own individual negative life experiences, we are all walking minefields where our emotional memory is concerned, and so is everyone else around you. None of us knows when we are going to say or do something that triggers someone else's emotional mines and have them blow up in our faces.

To return to the subject of the hapiym virus, the virus itself fed off the energies triggered by our emotions. It fed on the bioelectric and bio-magnetic emissions from our emotions. Not only did it feed on these energies; it learned to manipulate the body to magnify our emotions in order to increase its food supply. What we observe as human emotions are not the natural state of the 6th sense human emotional template, but are actually an artificially amplified, virus-instigated form of emotions. What science considers the human *norm* where our emotions are concerned is in fact the symptomatology of the residual effects of the hapiym mind virus infection itself. There are few people on this planet who have experienced the basic human template of human emotions without this tampering by the virus. The processes we teach about cellular clearing and self-deprogramming can remove these hyper-reactive emotional reactions and brings one to a more neutral operating state of emotional equanimity, what is often referred to as balance, or perhaps emotional stoicism. This is the natural state of human emotions, but living in a world where everyone's emotions have been artificially amplified by the hapiym virus infection, emotional equanimity appears as an aberration when compared to the infected emotions of the bodymind programmed by the virus infection. The symptoms of the infection are the accepted 'norm', and the norm is considered an oddity in comparison. How messed up is that?

In discussing this, I am only explaining emotions under normal circumstances as we understand and observe them. What happens when we have people who intentionally and knowingly tamper with our emotions for dastardly purposes? What I am proposing by this is not science fiction, but a very dark side of our current technological reality. The following chapters will unfold what is really happening in our world and to you beyond the scope of your knowledge or awareness. I suggest you buckle your seatbelt, because it gets very ugly from here forward.

10. Emotional Tampering and Mind Control

We are now going to step into the realm of the hidden world of tyranny in which you live with subliminal mind control warfare targeting you and your culture without your consent or awareness. This is not conspiracy fantasy, but reality. While everyone conjures up images of Chinese water torture and other methods to brainwash someone, the truth of what constitutes brainwashing and programming the public perception of reality is more sublime and despicable than you can imagine. Again, I am not sharing this horror story to frighten people, but to make them aware of what is being done to the public at large and how to free their consciousness from such tyrannical and subversive tactics of controlling the global population.

I have written in previous chapters how our perception of reality is a cognitive illusion. As such, there is some explanation required to define what a 'perceptual reality' is. A reality boils down to be an agreed upon consensus of a specific cultural narrative, or cultural story. The overarching reality of humanity is that we are physical beings living on a physical planet. We are each provided the equipment to navigate this physical and energetic environment with our senses and make of our lives what we can or choose to do. This is a definition of reality with which I think everyone can agree. This is the 'real' reality. We are all governed by what our senses teach us within this real aspect of reality. Beyond and below this real reality, we have multitudes of *perceptual* realities, realities based on accepted beliefs throughout our varied cultures worldwide.

Cultural realities are shaped by such things as traditions and beliefs. Cultures develop practices called traditions, and many of these traditions have been handed down from generation to generation for so long that no one knows their origin or reason, they just follow the practices because their forefathers did it and they are taught to emulate these practices as children. Few people question the cultural traditions into which they are born, they just continue the traditions and their practice as part of the accepted consensus norm because the rest of the culture agrees that it should be done because it has always been done that way. There is nothing in the real reality that mandates this continuance of traditions from ages past, so that makes cultural traditions nothing more than a continuing consensus *belief* that they should be maintained and enforced. For this reason, cultural realities are one of perception only, based on *belief* and practice alone and nothing more. It is an agreed-upon set of lies that continue because everyone agrees to adhere to the lies as a standard form of belief.

Every culture has its cultural lies, or what might more softly be referred to as cultural myths. To me it makes no difference, it is all a perceptual illusion and a mainstay of every culture around the planet. Within these cultural perceptual myths perceived as reality, we have many sub-realities such as religion, politics and history to sustain and/or work within the cultural perceptual framework. Each of these subsequent sub-realities is also predicated on an accepted illusion by specific groups of people who have agreed upon a consensus narrative to which they adhere and believe is reality. Again, these sub-realities are but perceptions based on nothing more than agreed-upon *beliefs*. They are narratives created by someone somewhere that a group of people can align themselves with by agreeing with the narrative and how it makes them feel emotionally. This belief doesn't have to have any basis in the real reality, it is only a belief based on an acceptance of whatever narrative they agree with and makes them feel good emotionally about their decision to accept the belief.

Every reality beneath the overarching reality is based on one narrative or another. The sub-realities are driven by stories concocted by someone somewhere along the line that had a more powerful story to gather people into a herd than another story may have done. Very often this narrative was enforced by force of arms. There may not be any real truth in these stories, but that doesn't matter, *believing* in the narrative is all that is required for one to acclimate to one narrative over another to shape the perceptual reality in which they choose to live their lives. The belief itself becomes the reality of the individual, and you dare not challenge another's beliefs because you are thereby challenging their personal perceptual reality, and ultimately the individual that embraces that belief.

When we embrace any beliefs, we make these beliefs a part of our personal identity, so to challenge the belief is to challenge the individual, or even the validity of the individual for having chosen an erroneous belief to shape the narrative of their personal reality. The hapiym virus was a fiction. It had no personality of its own but could only distinguish the specific infectious hive cells by copying and mimicking the personality of its human host. As such, it was always on the defensive, afraid of being discovered and eventually eradicated. The entire reality of the hapiym virus cell that lived within you was an illusion that was only substantiated on the belief that the virus cell *was* you. In order to maintain its control over your mind, it filled its (your) world with beliefs to sustain its own illusion of being something real. The virus itself had no personality, it was like an amoeba when it reproduced and infected its human host. It was a blank slate recording device that could only mimic, then later control its human host's personality by convincing us that the mimicked personality was actually us, so even our beliefs about ourselves are but a pale counterfeit of who we really are or what we can become as a human being. We have all bought the narrative of the virus.

I realize that this is hard to accept in a snapshot paragraph, but these explanations have been provided extensively in my other work for those interested in challenging this assertion, particularly the *Energetic War* book, to narrow down the scope of preliminary reading about the hapiym virus.

As reported previously, the hapiym virus was a hive mind. It could only function in a herd-like environment since it had no individuality of its own. It is because of this nature of the virus that human beings, who have all been infected with the virus habits, feel compelled to do everything in groups or herds. This virus hive compulsion to congregate in herds provides the foundational knowledge of why crowd psychology can be so accurate in forecasting how the human herds are liable to react to certain stimuli based on the particular narrative being driven by those who demand to control the human herds. If you can create a narrative that enough people will believe, you can create a new herd and drive that herd where you want it to go through cognitive and emotional manipulation. This type of herd management is all predicated on nothing more than establishing a *belief* in any specific narrative. You must have this foundational knowledge to be able to comprehend what is working behind the scenes to control humanity and ultimately rule the world.

The current triumvirate of power loosely referred to as the Deep State in modern vernacular, are only the latest perpetrators on the stage of controlling human consciousness. The will and drive to control humanity trace back to the ancient offworld gods, and this was all explained in depth in my three-volume subset of the *We Are Not Alone – Parts 1-3* books (WANA). Since the ancient offworld gods left the planet, there have been other store-minders left in their stead who have been manipulating humanity for the last 6,000 years. Simplistically you could refer to these people as the ruling elite. They are represented by all racial types all around the globe, not just specifically rich White men. Their ranks have been filled by the likes of Genghis Khan, Alexander the Great, the Roman Caesars, Aztec, Mayan and Inca rulers, as well as Pharaohs, kings and Popes throughout the ages. Today their ranks include the academic intelligentsia, as they have been since the Greek philosophers. More modern members of this cadre of elite overlords can be found in Hitler, Lenin, Stalin and any number of American Presidents. They fill the ranks of secret societies like the Freemasons, Rosicrucians, the Skull & Bones Society from Yale university, and the entire university fraternity system is but the training ground for these global elite and has been for more than a century.

Through a vast interconnected global network, the present triumvirate of power – the Fabian Society, Theosophical Society and SPR – once working in constant conflict with the Vatican, now have a Marxist Pope on St. Peter's throne as they work to consolidate all wealth and world power over humanity into their hands. Humanity, to these people, is nothing but the herds, the unwashed masses, the useless eaters. We are nothing but disposable goods in their quest for world domination. That is all humanity has ever been to these avaricious predators and they learned long ago how to control the unwashed masses through fictional narratives and false systems of belief – used time and again to send us off to useless wars, fighting and dying as a form of herd population control and to spread their own tribal superiority. These present controllers and their ancestors have been manipulating human emotions and human consciousness for the entire period of recorded human history, concocting false cultural myths and religions to pull the human herds together, then do with these herds as they see fit, laughing all the while as we continue generation after generation to take the bait of their contrived narratives and choose to die for them.

With this fundamental, yet troubling framework in hand, as disconcerting as it may be to your present sense of reality, we can now move forward into explaining how this form of cognitive tyranny is taking place in our technological era. From here forward it is going to get very deep conceptually, and I will have to take on the role of the translator to explain in layman's terms what the intellectual code-speak means in the following pages. The controlling elite of this planet have devised a form of intellectualist double-speak, meaning that what they say in their academic meanderings doesn't always reveal the meaning of their content unless one knows how to read through and decode the real meaning behind the intellectualist academic gobbledygook. Make no mistake, the high-fallutin' verbiage used by academics is there as a hidden weapon, often used by design to keep their sinister meaning out of reach of the 'uneducated' public. What may seem incomprehensible to the layman was designed for that exact purpose. Intellectualism was created as a cognitive barrier to keep the elite and their cadre separated and presumptively elevated above the ignorant masses as 'authorities'. Through such chicanery of language, the elite can and do present themselves as our superiors because they can speak the lingo of intellectualism and you are too stupid to follow the language of their bailiwick. It is just one more contrived trick to subjugate human consciousness.

In ages past, new narrative ideas were often spread by violence and forced capitulation to the new narrative ideology at the end of a sword. As much as many Christians don't want to face this fact, Christianity spread through violence and vandalism, destroying old pagan edifices, statues and burning libraries of learning. But for those Christians reading this, this is not an attack on Christianity, it is only a fact of history. Islam spread its doctrine at the point of a sword as well, as did the conquest of the global elite wherever they resided on the planet. Subjugation through terror and intimidation had been the rule more than the exception, and it is found wherever any ruling tyrannical elite came to power, from Montezuma and the Aztecs to the bloody revolutions of Marxism and Nazism. Forced conversion to religious or ideological narratives is not a new concept in the recorded annals of human history. Every ideological narrative that rises to a mass herd acceptance is punctuated with violence before all is said and done. This is irrefutable history.

With the advent of electronic technology, the ability to spread the word for mass psychological manipulation began with the invention of the radio. This ability to shape and mold human consciousness has only expanded as technological advances increased through television, computers and ultimately the internet. Whereas, in the beginning, this control took the form of ad jingoes that stuck in your mind, or music that preceded your favorite radio program, with television they were able to connect imagery with sound and create another level of cognitive control – think Operation Mockingbird. Through controlling the public narrative coupled with selected images, the news media could now direct the population's attention into any narrative rabbit hole it wanted the public to accept. Naturally, the public didn't realize that they were being psychologically manipulated with everything from ads to TV shows and sitcoms to news broadcasts. Hollywood movies have been a platform for public psychological control and narrative control since it started.

With the rise of social networks, people willingly participate on platforms, airing their personal dirty laundry, subject to emotional attacks by trolls and those who disagree with their personal opinions, and feeling that their value is measured by the number of likes they get on their posts or the number of associated 'friends' they can accumulate on their social network pages. We have seen a rise in the teen suicide rate over the issue of electronic cyber-bullying and unacceptance by their peer groups as a result of this emotional engagement in the world of the internet. Facebook has been forced to admit performing uninvited psychological experiments on a large number of its users without anyone being prosecuted for such psychological manipulation. With the rise and control of the Marxist left in the media and on the internet, we now face what is called shadow banning, aimed mostly at conservative opinions as a form of censorship to silence the voices of perhaps 50% of the population or more. The Fabian-controlled left-wing media produces 95% or more of the propagandized content it calls news to the public in order to sway and control public opinion to undermine a sitting president and possibly lead to a civil war in America once again. All of these are means to control the narrative that the Fabian Marxists want pushed to fulfill their objective of Globalist world domination. Yet these are only the apparent aspects of the psychological manipulation. Granted, these are all forms of cognitive mind control, but they are not the most sinister aspects of this agenda to control the human psyche. Enter Hendricus G. Loos and his technology, into whose work the next chapter will delve.

11. The Loos Devices and Emotional Frequency Control

All the information that precedes this chapter is fundamental to understanding what will be revealed here. This chapter is liable to be very technical until I offer my interpretations of the data. I can't help the technical nature of some of the information, but I ask the reader's forbearance in presenting the technical terminology so I can translate it into normal vernacular. By the time I am finished, despite all the technical language, the reader should come away with a basic understanding of what is taking place behind the technical language of the concepts shared herein.

It goes far beyond the scope of this book to try and explain the advances in neuroscience and what has been discovered about the bioelectric and bio-magnetic functions of the human body, but they should be a background consideration when deciphering the Loos information. Also keep in mind what I related about the human nervous system and emotional stimulation as a form of frequency response to our environment. Once I briefly cover some of these patents invented by Hendricus G. Loos, then I will explain how these patents are being used secretly against the public at large as a form of emotional control coupled with psychological manipulation to forward the dark Globalist agenda.

Electric fringe field generator for manipulating nervous systems

Patent number: 6081744

Abstract: **Apparatus and method for manipulating the nervous system of a subject through afferent nerves**, *modulated by externally applied weak fluctuating electric fields, tuned to certain frequencies* **such as to excite a resonance in neural circuits**. *Depending on the frequency chosen, excitation of such resonances causes in a human subject relaxation, sleepiness, sexual excitement, or the slowing of certain cortical processes. The electric field used for stimulation of the subject is induced by a pair of field electrodes charged to opposite polarity and placed such that* **the subject is entirely outside the space between the field electrodes. Such configuration allows for very compact devices where the field electrodes and a battery-powered voltage generator are contained in a small casing, such as a powder box.** *The stimulation by the weak external electric field relies on frequency modulation of spontaneous spiking patterns of afferent nerves.*

Type: Grant

Filed: July 17, 1998

Date of Patent: June 27, 2000

Inventor: Hendricus G. Loos

[Bold emphasis mine]

To translate this a bit more than what may be readily apparent, we have to know what afferent nerves are.

"Afferent neurons are sensory neurons that carry nerve impulses from sensory stimuli towards the central nervous system and brain, while efferent neurons are motor neurons that carry neural impulses away from the central nervous system and towards muscles to cause movement."

By this definition we learn that this particular Loos patent is designed to manipulate the nerves that lead to the brain as input stimuli by attacking the afferent nerves rather than the efferent part of the nervous system neural network. In the parlance of what I revealed in chapter 9 about the emotional sensory array being our nervous system, this Loos patent seeks to stimulate emotional reactions by an artificially induced "battery powered voltage generator" to stimulate the afferent nerve pathways to the brain. Hmm, can you say cell phone?

Subliminal acoustic manipulation of nervous systems
Patent number: 6017302
*Abstract: In human subjects, **sensory resonances can be excited by subliminal atmospheric acoustic pulses that are tuned to the resonance frequency**. The 1/2 Hz sensory resonance **affects the autonomic nervous system** and may cause relaxation, drowsiness, or sexual excitement, depending on the precise acoustic frequency near 1/2 Hz used. The effects of the 2.5 Hz*

resonance include slowing of certain cortical processes, sleepiness, and **disorientation**. *For these effects to occur,* ***the acoustic intensity must lie in a certain deeply subliminal range***. *Suitable apparatus consists of* ***a portable battery-powered source of weak subaudio acoustic radiation***. *The method and apparatus can be used by the general public as an aid to relaxation, sleep, or sexual arousal, and clinically for the control and perhaps treatment of insomnia, tremors, epileptic seizures, and anxiety disorders.*

Type: Grant

Filed: October 31, 1997

Date of Patent: January 25, 2000

Inventor: Hendricus G. Loos

[Bold emphasis mine]

What are these small subaudio delivery systems? Perhaps Walkmans or MP3 players, cell phones that can deliver subaudial signals through music or other audio sound generators like iPods, iPads or laptops? What the reader must realize from this is that these Loos frequencies can be delivered through many electromagnetic mediums. Being subaudio means that the signal is delivered subliminally below the normal human sound threshold and can be encoded in any other sound signature and you will never hear it or know that these frequencies are present and manipulating your emotional nervous system to someone else's demands.

Magnetic excitation of sensory resonances

Patent number: 5935054

*Abstract: The invention pertains to influencing the nervous system of a subject by a weak externally applied magnetic field with a frequency near 1/2 Hz. In a range of amplitudes, such fields can excite the 1/2 sensory resonance, **which is the physiological effect involved in "rocking the baby"**. The wave form of the stimulating magnetic field is restricted by conditions on the spectral power density, **imposed in order to avoid irritating the brain and the risk of kindling**. The method and apparatus can be used by the general public as an aid to relaxation, sleep, or arousal, and clinically for the control of tremors, seizures, and emotional disorders.*

Type: Grant

Filed: June 7, 1995

Date of Patent: August 10, 1999

Inventor: Hendricus G. Loos

[Bold emphasis mine]

What we are seeing with this is a form of artificially induced Alpha state. Our brains normally function at a higher Beta state when our attention is fully engaged. While in an Alpha state of awareness we are more susceptible to foreign input of information. Hypnotism functions on the Alpha state, so this Loos device lulls the subject into an artificially induced Alpha state making one more susceptible to subliminal programming by suggestion. In the Alpha state our mental guard is down, we are not functioning at our sharpest Beta state of awareness, and it is easier to slip in propagandized information while our normal waking awareness is lulled into this Alpha state of awareness. The Alpha state is a normal part of the human awareness usually encountered when we zone out while driving or that state or awareness just before we go to sleep. Every one of us at one time or another has drifted into the Alpha state, so this state of consciousness in and of itself is not a bad thing. But we have to wonder why Loos patented this device to artificially lull people into that state, which also occurs when we are brainlessly watching TV. When our cognitive guard is down, it is easier to plug in ideas and program our subconscious when our sharper Beta state is put to rest and we are less critical of the information delivered in the Alpha state.

In regard to 'kindling', it is most often referred to in the suppression of seizures with epilepsy, although its usage is controversial. Citing Wikipedia about the *Kindling Model* we are informed in part:

"The word kindling is a metaphor: the increase in response to small stimuli is similar to the way small burning twigs can produce a large fire. It is used by scientists to study the effects of repeated seizures on the brain. A seizure may increase the likelihood that more seizures will occur; an old saying in epilepsy research is "seizures beget seizures". Repeated stimulation "lowers the threshold" for more seizures to occur.

The brains of experimental animals **are repeatedly stimulated,** usually with electricity, to induce the seizures. Chemicals may also be used to induce seizures. The seizure that occurs after the first such electrical stimulation lasts a short time and is accompanied by a small amount of behavioral effects compared with seizures that result from repeated stimulations. With further seizures, the accompanying behavior intensifies, for example progressing from freezing in early stimulations to convulsions in later ones. The lengthening of duration and intensification of behavioral accompaniment eventually reaches a plateau after repeated stimulation. Even if animals are left unstimulated for as long as 12 weeks, the effect remains; the response to stimulation remains higher than it had been before."

"Already in the 1950s and 1960s, numerous authors recognized the seizure-inducing potential of focal stimulation. Here, Delgado and Sevillano demonstrated that repeated low-intensity stimuli to the hippocampus could lead to progressive increase of electrically evoked seizure activity. Yet, it was not until the late 1960s that Graham Goddard recognized the potential importance of this phenomenon and coined the term 'kindling'. Further research by Goddard on *the characteristics of the kindling phenomenon led to his conclusion that kindling can be used to model human epileptogenesis, **learning and memory**."*

[Bold emphasis mine]

What I personally take away from this, given the fact that we are mainly focused on stimulating the nervous system to create a certain emotional environment fertile for implanting mind control propaganda, is not the focus on epilepsy, but how this concept of 'kindling' can be used for 'learning and memory'. When one can artificially induce the alpha state and 'plug in' certain concepts of propagandized ideologies, then we have fertile ground to shape the consciousness of the target subjects. I realize to most readers that this may seem to be a reach and you may want to toss me into the fruitcake bin, but the fact is that Loos patented this device, along with others, to do things beyond what the patent specifications fully reveal to us. If this device was just about addressing seizures in epileptics, then why is he touting its usage by the general public in his patent abstract? As we progress with revealing more information, you will have the chance to decide for yourself whether this is all looney tunes or whether our culture has been under serious psychological and emotional assault or not. This particular Loos device is designed to avoid the kindling associated with creating seizures, and I will suggest its design is geared more to inducing the Alpha state of awareness to make the individual more susceptible to subliminal programming, or shall we say, "learning and memory".

Manipulation of nervous systems by electric fields

Patent number: 5899922

Abstract: Apparatus and method for **manipulating the nervous system of a subject through afferent nerves, modulated by an externally applied weak electric field. The field frequency is to be chosen such that the modulation causes excitation of a sensory resonance.** *The resonances found so far include one near 1/2 Hz which affects the autonomic nervous system, and a resonance near 2.4 Hz that causes* **slowing of certain cortical processes.** *Excitation of the 1/2 Hz autonomic resonance causes relaxation, sleepiness, ptosis of the eyelids, or sexual excitement, depending on the precise frequency used. The weak electric field for causing the excitation is applied to skin areas away from the head of the subject, such as to avoid substantial polarization current densities in the brain. Very weak fields suffice for bringing about the physiological effects mentioned.* **This makes it possible to excite sensory resonances with compact battery powered devices that have a very low current consumption.**

Type: Grant

Filed: November 14, 1997

Date of Patent: May 4, 1999

Inventor: Hendricus G. Loos

[Bold emphasis mine]

Afferent nerve stimulation again to create emotional frequency resonance through 'compact battery powered devices.' Cell phones? It is obvious that Loos designed these patents to be in the hands of the public and had the desire that these products be available to the public as tools to manipulate their emotional sensory array through the nervous system manipulation and artificially induced resonance. If these devices were for strictly clinical usage, then why create 'low power battery units' which is highly suggestive of some kind of portable device? When this patent was approved in 1999, cell phone technology was at best in its infancy. If you look at our world cultures today, we see most of the population addicted to cell phone use. Is the explosion of cell phone usage (including free government giveaways) merely about convenience, or is there a more sinister purpose behind their design and wide distribution given what we know about the Loos patents? One thing is certain. Billions of people worldwide are carrying around 'compact battery powered devices' attached to their head virtually all of their waking hours. Coincidence?

NERVOUS SYSTEM MANIPULATION BY ELECTROMAGNETIC FIELDS FROM MONITORS

Publication number: 20020188164

Abstract: Physiological effects have been observed in a human subject in response to stimulation of the skin with weak electromagnetic fields that are pulsed with certain frequencies near ½ Hz or 2.4 Hz, such as to excite a sensory resonance. Many computer monitors and TV tubes, when displaying pulsed images, emit pulsed electromagnetic fields of sufficient amplitudes to cause such excitation. It is therefore possible to manipulate the nervous system of a subject by pulsing images displayed on a nearby computer monitor or TV set. For the latter, the image pulsing may be imbedded in the program material, or it may be overlaid by modulating a video stream, either as an RF signal or as a video signal. The image displayed on a computer monitor may be pulsed effectively by a simple computer program. For certain monitors, pulsed electromagnetic fields capable of exciting sensory resonances in nearby subjects may be generated even as the displayed images are pulsed with subliminal intensity.

Type: Application
Filed: June 1, 2001
Publication date: December 12, 2002
Inventor: Hendricus G. Loos

There is no point in highlighting any segment of this patent. Everything you need to know about emotional nervous system stimulation is covered in this particular patent. When you consider the CIA's Operation Mockingbird coupled with this Loos technology, then you can see exactly how the public has been programmed through subliminal frequency modulation through everything from TVs to dumb computer CRT terminals to modern PCs and laptops. Through pulsed signals on all these devices, the Loos frequencies have been used to manipulate public opinion by generating emotional outrage over specific incidents presented on the news, which is particularly in play today by the television media on both sides. The current 'Hate Trump' agenda being pushed by the left is a prime example of emotional manipulation through media propaganda. How much of this instilled hatred is artificially induced by Loos technology and subliminal signals targeting the public's nervous system to incite such violent emotions when coupled with Hate Trump rhetoric spewed out by the Mockingbird press? There are other factors to consider which I will cover in the next chapter insofar as this public brainwashing goes.

As the patent says, with the subliminal frequencies "the image pulsing may be imbedded in the program material, or it may be overlaid by modulating a video stream, either as an RF signal or as a video signal". What this means is that everything you watch or look at on a computer or TV screen has the potential of carrying embedded Loos frequencies to mess with your emotions while you view whatever it is you are looking at on your computer monitor or TV. The pulsing does not require video streaming to carry the Loos frequencies and the frequencies can be embedded on pages that are text only on the internet just as easily as they can be with streaming video or strictly audio presentations.

There is a more sinister side to all of this where YouTube video content is concerned, and I will cover that as we progress. For now, I think I have provided more than enough disconcerting information for the reader to digest regarding how you are and have been emotionally manipulated for at least two decades through Loos technology and those people who have a specific agenda to keep you cowed and subdued. At some point we all have to move beyond simple denial of these facts because they don't happen to support our own narrative belief system and accept this as real reality. I told you this was going to be a rough ride, and it's not over yet.

12. Associative Memory and Brainwashing

I have a confession to make. When I started this book a few weeks ago I had a certain direction I intended to take it, but by the time I completed Chapter 7, I abandoned the project feeling that it would probably not be read by those who most needed to read the material in this book (just about everyone on the planet). The book sat idle for at least three weeks and I was disinclined to finish the book in the format I originally planned to present the material.

I don't work from outlines when I write my books, they usually write themselves and unfold in the manner that they do based on what you might call inspiration and insight, often being prompted by finding something in my continual research that prompts me to write a book. I don't make a habit of sitting around dreaming up book projects to do. They take a lot of time, effort and research and it is hard work writing, editing and self-publishing them. But when my muse strikes, I have little choice other than to follow the 'push' and write what wants to come out of me. What turned the tide on this book and set me back on the path to completing it was rereading the Loos patents and discovering the one I will discuss in this chapter. After reading this particular patent and about 20 minutes of hard research, I realized where I had to take this book to get it where it needed to go.

I didn't originally intend to reveal all the information I have presented thus far in this volume, as it was conceived for a mainstream 'first cognition' audience. It was not my intent to dive into the conspiracy rabbit hole for the simple reason that most people are so put off by the word conspiracy that they are likely not to read this book if it was presented as a conspiracy tome. But when I discovered the Loos patent that I will discuss here, and the subsequent information it led me to, there was no way I could deliver the full understanding to any audience about the tyranny of emotionally generated mind control without telling the whole story. Lacking the overall fundamental background to serve as a foundation for understanding the thrust of this volume, it would have made no sense. There would have been too many holes to make the presentation cogent. When I looked into the Loos patent about Associative Memory, and did the subsequent research, I knew I had to tell the whole story, even if it was in a synopsized abbreviated form, or the full understanding of this material would not be possible.

The more I looked at what I wanted to present, the more I realized that the story about the hapiym virus had to be included in the fundamental knowledge category. As challenging as such a concept may be to a cold reader, it still had to be presented in book, along with a keen understanding of the global conspiracy to subjugate all humanity or reporting the whys of Loos developing his technologies would have no meaning. Although I have covered all the topical matter more extensively in my other books, I realized that the reader would not be able to make heads or tails about emotionalism if they didn't at least have a synopsized overview of the whole shebang. One will not see the whole tapestry looking at only one small corner of it and seeking to understand what the full picture of the tapestry is. Therefore, this book changed course and morphed into what it is out of necessity.

Method and apparatus for associative memory

Patent number: 5995954

Abstract: A method and apparatus for an electronic artificial neural network, which serves as an associative memory that has a complete set of N-dimensional Hadamard vectors as stored states, suitable for large N that are powers of 2. The neural net has nonlinear synapses, each of which processes signals from two neurons. These synapses can be implemented by simple passive circuits comprised of eight resistors and four diodes. The connections in the neural net are specified through a subset of a group that is defined over the integers from 1 to N. The subset is chosen such that the connections can be implemented in VLSI or wafer scale integration. An extension of the Hadamard memory causes the memory to provide new Hadamard vectors when these are needed for the purpose of Hebb learning.

Type: Grant

Filed: March 18, 1992

Date of Patent: November 30, 1999

Inventor: Hendricus G. Loos

At first glance this may seem to be strictly electronics talk, especially when we see terms like resistors, diodes and VLSI referenced. VLSI is:

> *"Very-large-scale integration (VLSI) is the process of creating an integrated circuit (IC) by combining hundreds of thousands of transistors or devices into a single chip. VLSI began in the 1970s when complex semiconductor and communication technologies were being developed. The microprocessor is a VLSI device."*

If you think I have stretched your imagination limits thus far in this book, you ain't seen nothin' yet. You are about to have your imagination stretched to capacity. From this patent the first place I looked was *Associative Memory (psychology)* on Wikipedia where I found:

> *"In psychology, associative memory is defined as the ability to learn and remember the relationship between unrelated items. This would include, for example, remembering the name of someone or the aroma of a particular perfume.* ***This type of memory deals specifically with the relationship between these different objects or concepts.*** *A normal associative memory task involves testing participants on their recall of pairs of unrelated items, such as face-name pairs.*

Associative memory is a declarative memory structure and episodically based."

"Two important processes for learning associations, and thus forming associative memories, are **operant conditioning** *and classical conditioning. Operant conditioning refers to a type of learning where* **behavior is controlled by environmental factors that influence the behavior of the subject in subsequent instances of the stimuli***. In contrast, classical conditioning is when a response is conditioned to an unrelated stimulus."*

[Bold emphasis mine]

I am going to share my path of research then I will weave all these components together into a cohesive whole. Once I found this definition of associative memory, then I looked into *Operant Conditioning* on Wikipedia and discovered:

"Operant conditioning (also called instrumental conditioning) is a learning process through which **the strength of a behavior is modified by reinforcement or punishment. It is also a procedure that is used to bring about such learning.**

*Although operant and classical conditioning both involve behaviors controlled by environmental stimuli, they differ in nature. **In operant conditioning, stimuli present when a behavior is rewarded or punished come to control that behavior**. For example, a child may learn to open a box to get the sweets inside, or learn to avoid touching a hot stove; in operant terms, the box and the stove are "discriminative stimuli". Operant behavior is said to be "voluntary": for example, the child may face a choice between opening the box and petting a puppy."*

[Bold emphasis mine]

From operant conditioning I then looked into what the Loos patent referred to as Hebb learning and found an explanation on Wikipedia under *Hebbian theory:*

*"Hebbian theory is a neuroscientific theory claiming that an increase in synaptic efficacy arises from a **presynaptic cell's** repeated and persistent stimulation of a postsynaptic cell. **It is an attempt to explain synaptic plasticity, the adaptation of brain neurons during the learning process**. It was introduced by Donald Hebb in his 1949 book* The Organization of Behavior. *The theory is also called Hebb's rule, Hebb's postulate, and cell assembly theory. Hebb states it as follows:*

*"**Let us assume that the persistence or repetition of a reverberatory activity (or "trace") tends to induce lasting cellular changes that add to its stability. ... When an axon of cell A is near enough to excite a cell B and repeatedly or persistently takes part in firing it, some growth process or metabolic change takes place in one or both cells such that A's efficiency, as one of the cells firing B, is increased.**"*

*The theory is often summarized as "**Cells that fire together wire together**." This summary, however, should not be taken too literally. Hebb emphasized that **cell A needs to "take part in firing" cell B, and such causality can occur only if cell A fires just before, not at the same time as, cell B.** This important aspect of causation in Hebb's work foreshadowed what is now known about spike-timing-dependent plasticity, which requires temporal precedence.*

*The theory attempts to explain associative or Hebbian learning, in which simultaneous activation of cells leads to pronounced increases in synaptic strength between those cells. It also provides a **biological** basis for errorless learning methods for education and memory rehabilitation.*

[Bold emphasis mine]

You are probably thoroughly confused over where I might be going with all this technical neuroscientific jargon, but it will all weave together into a comprehensive whole of understanding before I'm done. To read through and understand where all this technical talk goes, one must have a working model, or at least a framework of understanding in which to place these principles to comprehend what is being proposed behind ideas like Hebbian learning and operant conditioning.

When we read Loos' patent in this context, it is rather obvious that he is talking about the design of an integrated circuit, but where the masking of his intent is concerned is where he uses the word *Method* in his patent to initiate this form of Hebbian learning. So now we have to delve a little bit into the background of Donald O. Hebb. Although not yet mentioned in this work, in my earlier works I explained to people that whenever you turn over a rock you will eventually find a connection to Theosophy, the Fabians or the SPR. Looking into Hebb's biographical information on Wikipedia, low and behold we find another Theosophical connection. As Wikipedia informs us:

"Donald's parents were both medical doctors. Donald's mother was heavily influenced

by the ideas of Maria Montessori, and she home-
schooled him until the age of 8."

From my own prior research, I knew that Maria Montessori, who was the founder of the Montessori schools, was steeped in Theosophy. The link below, which leads to an article entitled *Montessori and the Theosophical Society* put out by the Theosophical Society, leaves no room for arguing this fact.

https://www.theosophical.org/publications/quest-magazine/42-publications/quest-magazine/1409-montessori-and-the-theosophical-society

What we learn from this is that Hebb was raised in an environment steeped in Theosophical ideas. His field of expertise was psychology, so any designs by Hendricus G. Loos using the Hebbian model for learning are predicated on psychological manipulation, not strictly AI and computer chips. Because there is such a dearth of information on Loos, I have not been able to find any connection between him and the Fabians or the Theosophical Society, but instinct tells me that there probably is one given the information that will be revealed as we move ahead.

Before putting the ribbon on this box, we have to touch briefly on 'spike-timing-dependent plasticity' (STDP). Wikipedia provides these explanations about STDP:

"Spike-timing-dependent plasticity (STDP)
*is **a biological process that adjusts the strength of***

connections between neurons in the brain. The process adjusts the connection strengths based on the relative timing of a particular neuron's output and input action potentials (or spikes). The STDP process partially explains the activity-dependent development of nervous systems, especially with regard to long-term potentiation and long-term depression."

*"Under the STDP process, **if an input spike to a neuron tends, on average, to occur immediately before that neuron's output spike, then that particular input is made somewhat stronger**. If an input spike tends, on average, to occur immediately after an output spike, then that particular input is made somewhat weaker hence: "spike-timing-dependent plasticity". Thus, **inputs that might be the cause of the post-synaptic neuron's excitation are made even more likely to contribute in the future**, whereas inputs that are not the cause of the post-synaptic spike are made less likely to contribute in the future. The process continues until a subset of the initial set of connections remain, while the influence of all others is reduced to 0. Since a neuron produces an output spike when many of its inputs occur within a brief period, the subset of inputs that remain are those that tended to be correlated in time. In*

addition, **since the inputs that occur before the output are strengthened, the inputs that provide the earliest indication of correlation will eventually become the final input to the neuron.***"*

[Bold emphasis mine]

To pull the final technical pieces of this puzzle together we have to look at what is known as the Walsh-Hadamard Transformation. In an article abstract entitled *"Towards holographic "brain" memory based on randomization and Walsh-Hadamard transformation."* We find this information:

"The holographic conceptual approach to cognitive processes in the human brain suggests that, in some parts of the brain, each part of the memory (a neuron or a group of neurons) contains some information regarding the entire data. *In Dolev and Frenkel (2010, 2012)* **we demonstrated how to encode data in a holographic manner using the Walsh-Hadamard transform.** *The encoding is performed on randomized information, that is then represented by a set of Walsh-Hadamard coefficients. These coefficients turn out to have holographic properties. Namely,* **any portion of the set of coefficients defines a "blurry image" of the original data. In this work, we describe a built-in error correction technique**--*enlarging the width of* *the matrix used in the Walsh-Hadamard transform to produce a rectangular Hadamard matrix.* **By adding this redundancy, the data can bear more errors, resulting in a system that is not affected by missing coefficients up to a certain threshold. Above this threshold, the loss of data is reflected by getting a "blurry image" rather than a concentrated damage.** *We provide a heuristic analysis of the ability of the technique to correct errors, as well as an example of an image saved using the system. Finally, we give an example of a simple implementation of our approach using neural networks as a proof of concept."*

[Bold emphasis mine]

https://www.ncbi.nlm.nih.gov/pubmed/26945440

The last piece of this puzzle resides in the concept of Groupthink. From an article in *Psychology Today* entitled *What is Groupthink?* we are informed:

"Groupthink occurs when a group of well-intentioned people make irrational or non-optimal decisions that are spurred by the urge to conform or the discouragement of dissent."

https://www.psychologytoday.com/us/basics/groupthink

Additionally, Wikipedia informs us about *Groupthink* as follows:

"Groupthink is a psychological phenomenon that occurs within a group of people in which the desire for harmony or conformity in the group results in an irrational or dysfunctional decision-making outcome. Group members try to minimize conflict and reach a consensus decision without critical evaluation of alternative viewpoints by actively suppressing dissenting viewpoints, and by isolating themselves from outside influences.

Groupthink requires individuals to avoid raising controversial issues or alternative solutions, and there is loss of individual creativity, uniqueness and independent thinking. The dysfunctional group dynamics of the "ingroup" produces an "illusion of invulnerability" (an inflated certainty that the right decision has been made). Thus the "ingroup" significantly overrates its own abilities in decision-making and significantly underrates the abilities of its opponents (the "outgroup"). Furthermore, groupthink can produce dehumanizing actions against the "outgroup".

With all this information now in hand we can assemble all these pieces into a comprehensive whole of understanding. The 'method' of learning that Loos suggested in the patent that opened this chapter is a form of reinforced learning, creating a 'holographic' mind (groupthink) through artificially introducing electronic signals to the nervous system to create the STDP effect by exciting the input neuron endings to create programmed behavior as output with a lasting associative memory effect.

The 'blurry image' referenced in the Walsh-Hadamard Transformation could be any image that could be used as trigger using Loos technologies to artificially stimulate the nervous system to create the STDP spike to create an associative memory based on emotional stimulation with a lasting psychological outcome for the long term through memory association.

What sparked my investigation was in watching the programmed behavior of the leftist ideologues, particularly on college campuses, and how they are all emotional basket cases, and also how their rigid groupthink mentality keeps them blind from any alternative idea beyond their brainwashed world narrative. As a simple example, let's say that you have a room full of college students, perhaps an auditorium filled to capacity for a lecture. Let's assume that the lecture is on political science or environmentalism. Through the course of this lecture the students are shown images of perhaps baby seals being clubbed to death on arctic ice, with the vibrant red blood splattered all over the ice, or perhaps images of places like Chernobyl and the environmental devastation after that incident.

To create an emotional associative memory, one only needs to embed a Loos frequency into these images to create that STDP spike in the brain's neurons to trigger specific emotional responses through the CNS. The emotional frequency could be one that induces horror or any number of negative reinforcement emotional signals. Through artificially attacking the nervous system via Loos frequencies, then showing these images, the students will then have the 'blurry image' of the Walsh-Hadamard Transformation to serve as that associative emotional reminder. Because they have had their input afferent neurons artificially stimulated, as the Walsh-Hadamard Transformation coefficient states, it creates a stronger output signal creating more long-lasting memories based on the 'blurry image' associated with the input spike on the neurons in the brain through Loos frequency manipulation,

When you couple this type of artificially induced neural shock from Loos frequencies attacking the central nervous system to induce the desired emotional frequency response along with propagandized Marxist ideologies on environmentalism, political concepts, hate Trump, hate Christians, aversion to MAGA hats and embed specific emotional triggers that create a false sense of artificially induced outrage, then you have created a holographic group mind.

Following the Hebbian model, you can then not only align the neurons in the brain to think and react in the same manner to the same stimuli through associative memory. Using observant conditioning within the groupthink framework, you can create a mass 'holographic mind' made up of individual human robots programmed in the same manner to be turned into a brainless army of violent drones, subject to the whims of their programmers. Through such means the controllers have created an army of unthinking drones, what the communists call useful idiots, to serve as agents of terror against a target population. As noted in the information about groupthink, the sense of individuality and critical thinking is lost in the morass of the groupthink narrative, whether that narrative has any basis in reality or not.

When one reads all the information shared in this chapter without a comparative context, it all sounds innocent and scientific, yet all these principles, with the exception of Loos creating a computer chip with this particular patent, are based on psychological and neurological studies of *biological* units – i.e. human brain and nervous system studies. Everything Loos tried to accomplish with his computer chips is based on psychological manipulation of the human nervous system, tampering with neural input signals to the brain, and creating a human 'holographic mind' resulting in what we observe in our cultures as Marxist groupthink. It is one of the most sinister forms of mind control and brainwashing imaginable and it goes completely unnoticed by the public. And it is all achieved primarily through emotional manipulation by intentionally artificially triggering emotional responses in the human nervous system by the Loos technologies. Introduction of the Loos frequencies that attack the CNS provide the input 'spike' to the presynaptic neurons embedding the primary emotional programming coupled with the images used to formulate the more long-lasting associative memory on the post-synaptic memory output. The subsequent addition of specifically formulated propaganda, once the brain cells have been assaulted and stimulated through CNS manipulation, creates the 'blurry image' association with the triggered emotional response, and the propaganda fed to the target audience immediately thereafter creates the desired emotional output, i.e. anger, hatred, fear, etc.

Similar forms of mind control have been used throughout the ages with Eastern religions using mantras to put the Beta mind to sleep, catechisms and recitations in churches and other repetitious rituals to dull the mind and make it open to suggestion, or fear excitation through fire and brimstone sermons graphically preaching the penalties of Hell. With the advent of modern technology, these ancient practices are made easier through artificially stimulating the emotional frequencies of the nervous system and then filling the heads of the targeted population with propaganda to create almost any false reality narrative they want accepted by their target audience. I used the Marxist left as my example in this chapter because those who are indoctrinated with the ideology are the easiest to identify to the public at large at the present time.

Once the 'blurry image' created through the emotional reactions is established, all sorts of seemingly unrelated 'causes' can be attached to that core emotional image and simply folded into the associative memory, whether there is any direct association or not. The 'blurry image' of the emotional trigger is all that is required to attach anything else to it. Through operant conditioning and group reinforcement through groupthink, the programming only embeds deeper into the psyche strengthening the programming. Once this deep emotional associative memory is in place, everyone who is not in the 'ingroup' is automatically the 'outgroup' and must be eliminated. This type of irrational associative illogic is why you see so many Marxist drones proclaiming peace and equality, save the whales and save the planet, all while screaming to tear down and destroy anyone who disagrees with their ideological groupthink. We love peace, but if you disagree with us, we will kill you or destroy you!

With the constant repetitious Marxist diatribe spewed out by the Mockingbird media to reinforce this psychological programming, and a cadre of political agitators and anarchists to rile up the ranks of the groupthink ingroup, we have a recipe for tragedy in the making.

13. Creating False Narratives

With all the information presented thus far in this book, you are now ready to see more of the picture where emotional mind control is being applied beyond what has already been shared. We are going to jump into the YouTube arena and also discuss a bit more about social networks to show you how pervasive this emotional control permeates our technological culture.

As previously stated, before psychological control can be most effective, there has to be an emotional element factored in to create the psychological disruption. Whether this emotional factor is produced by peer pressure, repetitive rituals that dull the mind, elements of fear or whatever emotion can be induced to implant ideas in the consciousness, emotions still lie at the foundation of all brainwashing. If you take a genuinely objective view of religious rituals, you will notice that hymns and other ritualistic devices also serve as a catalyst to set an emotional trigger. Just look at the how people react to *Amazing Grace*, or *Just as I am* and the emotional responses they evoke, or the emotions generated by hymns like *Onward, Christian Soldiers*! Also look at how Muslims react to prayer call, or Jews bobbing before the Wailing Wall. Each of these situations bring forth an emotional response, as do holiday rituals, and the list goes on.

The hapiym mind virus fed itself through artificially amplifying human emotions. Not only did it thrive on the emotions it could make its host body produce, but it also fed on the emotional energies of others in our surrounding environment. Remember the bioelectric bubble that every human being emits as part of our body's emotional sensory array, and then expand that to the view that every human being is walking around with these energetic bubbles rubbing against each other whenever we meet other people, whether individually or in crowds. When you can expand your perception to see all these bubbles of energy interfacing virtually all the time, then you can see what an energetically toxic environment in which we live with everyone's emotional bioelectric bubble rubbing against everyone else's.

It is through such field interactions that crowds at concerts get emotional highs when a band plays their favorite songs. The amplified ebullience from the crowd environment infects every person individually and each person experiences an emotional 'high' from this group field interaction. In like kind, a group field interface in a situation like a mass shooting also infects a crowd with panic, and the emotion of fear is equally transmitted through the bioelectric environment even if an individual in close proximity doesn't yet know what is taking place and is confused. Their body reacts because of the group bioelectric field interaction before the brain in some cases even knows what is taking place. It is this group energetic field interaction that creates the contagion of mobs and mob violence.

Because the hapiym virus was a hive intelligence, everyone infected with the virus already had what you could call a sympathetic resonance with another person or group infected with the virus. Humans are social animals, like wolf packs, but it was the hapiym hive virus that *socialized* our species. The definition of socialized illustrates this:

*"having been **made to behave** in a way that is acceptable to a particular society."*

The energetic nature of the hive mind virus linked everyone together through this interactive biomagnetic field, which served as the transmission and receiving platform for the emotional energies on which the virus itself fed and which artificially *socialized* the entire human species into the hive/herd mentality of the virus against its will. This is why groupthink and shared belief narratives have the power that they do over our consciousness. The herding instinct of the virus itself drives humanity into socialized clusters, or hives, and these hives are predicated on the sympathetic energetic resonance produced by the virus symptomatology coupled with shared systems of beliefs, or narratives. At our current level of cognitive development, based on residual hive infection symptomatology, it is the rare individual indeed that can function outside one herd narrative or another. Also, these varied herds are almost always exclusivist in nature, with one's personal herd narrative being superior to all others who may share a similar yet differing variant of the same herd narrative. Every herd feels superior to all others without fail, and every herd defends their narrative against any and all others, creating another form of groupthink to reinforce their individual narrative belief system.

As an independent biological unit with an individual personality, our species has fought against this herding instinct because it reduces the individual to nothing more than a herd beast based on the hive infection. Each human being is designed to be an autonomous unit at its base level of programming of individualism, yet the hapiym mind virus created friction with this base programming by seeking to turn us all to *its* mandate of hive structuring, creating a constant inner conflict where, on one hand we beat our breast about being an individual, yet on the other we demand that others that we associate with think like we do – i.e. demanding to associate with like-minded individuals. This is why, at the present time, we have a divided consciousness where we have a true ego (the primary autonomous unit programming) and a false ego produced by the hive (which causes the demand to herd together in clusters of socialized, like-minded individuals). Based on the virus infection, we are all sort of schizophrenic in this regard, and this is why I can make the statement that you don't know who you are.

When the virus infected us, it did its utmost to reprogram the autonomous human form by programming the bodymind, particularly the nervous system and the emission of emotional energies, so it could keep itself fed. It took the fundamental nervous system emotional capabilities and artificially amplified our emotions to fulfill its feeding requirements. The virus was an emotional energy junkie, and as a result of countless generations of this infection, we have all become emotion junkies because of how the virus programmed the bodymind and our nervous system to react to *its* designs. This is why I say that science and psychology have failed humanity by classifying these infected programmed and amplified emotional responses as the human norm. The truth is that, as a general rule, we do not know what the human norm is where our emotions are concerned because all we know is the artificially amplified emotions the virus programmed our bodies with. This is why our emotions run from the highest of highs to the lowest of lows, what we refer to as the emotional rollercoaster.

Because the virus thrived on our emotional emissions, we have all been heavily programmed to seek emotional gratification where our beliefs are concerned. When we latch onto a belief and it can deliver an emotional high or a sense of contentment, we are psychologically cowed into accepting whatever programming fulfills this emotional gratification. The psychologists have figured out this part of presumed human nature where our emotions are concerned, even if they haven't figure out why we seek this reward gratification.

Through accepting any belief, no matter what it is, the vast majority of the population seeks continual reinforcement of their beliefs. This is called confirmation bias, and every belief system requires confirmation bias to support the belief. Most people do not want to hear anything that might undermine their beliefs, so they deny what they find that opposes or questions their beliefs, and instead turn to finding information that bolsters their belief through confirmation bias and narrative reinforcement. Through this form of psychological reinforcement, the virus held our consciousness captive to its desires to find that emotional gratification whenever we found anything that confirmed our belief system and gave us that emotional reward. In like kind, once a narrative belief system was adopted, the virus programmed us to react with fear or dread when anything challenged its accepted belief narrative to keep us locked into any specific narrative. The virus used its own form of operant conditioning of emotional punishment and reward to keep us all in line with its desires. This sense of emotional reward is what keeps the belief in place and only strengthened the belief illusion. As noted in the groupthink passage in the last chapter, all groupthink is reinforced either through reward or punishment. This is true of every mass belief on the planet, although it can be more hateful within certain ideologies when it is perpetrated intentionally than with others. Every group belief on the planet is part of the hapiym hive programming, and the virus was extremely exclusivist between each ingroup and their outgroups. This is where different narratives and subrealities come into the picture.

Because people have different interests, the Fabian-Theosophy-SPR networks worldwide have created think tanks where people are paid high fees to sit around and devise new narratives when part of the public starts to reject old narratives (programming). I realize that accepting such a notion may challenge your worldview, but you must ask why narratives like the flat earth have gained such traction in the marketplace, and its adherents are as rabid as any other religious zealot in defending that belief system. Where did such an idea come from, and how has it grown such a strength of followers in a relatively short time?

We find our answer when we look at propaganda videos promoting the flat earth ideology which have been embedded with Loos frequencies to make people accept the belief by stimulating their nervous system. Taking the example provided in the last chapter, a calculating subversive can create a well-made video production pushing an idea like flat earth, then use the Loos frequencies to embed the belief through subliminal nervous system tampering. I am not putting this idea out here as theoretical positing, I am telling you this is fact. When you have agencies like the unholy triumvirate with virtually unlimited finances, you can create a wealth of videos and bombard the YouTube marketplace with Loos frequency-embedded productions to push forward whatever agenda you want, create any narrative you want. All you need is the click bait to attract your target audience into your clutches and a new belief system can be spawned.

I am providing a link to a 4-hour presentation called *The Century of Self* available on YouTube in the link below. If any reader doubts the psychological manipulation against humanity I profess in this book, then I highly recommend watching this production. It was originally four 1-hour segments that have all been strung together into a single presentation. This particular production validates everything I revealed in *The Psychology of Becoming Human* and provides added details which I didn't cover in that book.

https://www.youtube.com/watch?v=eJ3RzGoQC4s

The arena of modern spirituality, loosely referred to as the New Age, was an invention of psychologists closely associated with the Fabian Society and the Theosophical Society, and it was launched at Esalen Institute in Big Sur, California during the heyday of the sex, drugs and rock & roll era of the 1960s. It is admittedly the acknowledged launching point for the entire New Age spiritual revolution as I covered at length in some of our other works like *Revamping Psychology*. The documentary, *The Century of Self* fully validates what we presented in that book and others.

New age spirituality is a goulash of beliefs all cobbled together, folding in beliefs from Hindu and Buddhist religious concepts, ideas about neo-shamanism based on the fictional stories concocted by Carlos Castenada (who also spoke at Esalen Institute), professing ideas about expanding your consciousness through using psychedelics advocated by the Fabian Society member Aldous Huxley (author of *Brave New World*) and Timothy Leary; cobbled together with UFOlogy, escapist notions about aliens coming to save humanity, or other fanciful notions about Ascending to the 5th dimension to ultimately wake up on a New Earth. The concept of the 5th dimension is straight out of the writings of Madame Blavatsky and the Theosophical Society. When looking at the goulash of beliefs loosely attached to New Age ideologies, remember the associative memory aspect of unrelated ideas being harnessed together through that 'blurry image' concept.

To harness people more firmly into this Theosophical spiritual fraud, YouTube is loaded with videos about people raising their vibration or alleged DNA activations which will allegedly make someone more spiritually attuned. Coupled with these concepts of the docility doctrine of Love and Light, there is no shortage of click bait on YouTube to attract people to these videos seeking spiritual gratification. Enter Loos frequency tampering.

When people dial into these lures for their consciousness, the Loos frequencies attack the CNS and can artificially induce the feeling of love on the emotional spectrum, or they can agitate the CNS to feel more energetic temporarily (raising your vibration). Through such fraudulent means of frequency manipulation, people are drawn into the spiritual myth that they are actually raising their vibration or feeling the love of God or the cosmos. Such tactics are also used on spiritual websites embedded in doctrinal text pages, as well as on angel videos or other alleged spiritual videos where people are hoodwinked into thinking they are finding something of spiritual value when they get the Loos-induced love jolt embedded in these presentations. Christian propaganda of a similar nature is not exempt from such frequency manipulation either.

Although the Loos patents shared in this book paint frequency modulation of the CNS to produce reactions of relaxation, you can rest assured that experimentation has taken place where the unholy triumvirate knows the full emotional bioelectric spectrum and knows exactly how to trigger any emotional response they desire.

There is a wealth of End Times videos to cater to the Christian public and many of these presentations are also laden with Loos frequencies of varied natures, with some causing fear and anxiety over a coming tribulation, and sometimes coupled with the hope of Jesus' immediate return. Into this mix you can also throw prophecy videos as well.

The conspiracy marketplace has been dominated by the triumvirate since the 90s, and it really spread with YouTube going public in 2005, serving as one of the greatest propaganda mind control platforms ever devised outside mainstream media. Many of the conspiracy videos, particularly those put out by people like David Icke, Michael Tsarion, David Wilcock and Mark Passio, are an admixture of partial historical conspiracy facts coupled with heavy doses of Theosophical mystical beliefs and propaganda. Each of these named conspiracy commentators have affiliations with the Theosophical Society and its ideologies. They each may put their own individual spin on this information to gain market share, but they all spring from the same Theosophical doctrinal cesspool and it takes little investigation to bear this out – usually admitted in their own videos. Into this mix you can throw hundreds of other alleged psychics and channelers, most of whom are also agents for the triumvirate network spreading the good word of cognitive docility, love & light.

On the flipside of all this, we find the 'controlled opposition' of alleged right wing and neo-Nazi videos, also laden with Loos frequency signatures to generate fear and anger in order to try and start a civil war in America. It is all placed there by specific design to sow dissent and keep opposing poles at each other's throats to create cultural disruption. This is coupled with many leftist YouTube channels using the same energies to play on people's emotions through paranoia and fear. At the root of all of this lies emotional manipulation, abused as the platform to plug in psychological doctrinal programming of whatever the video producers can concoct to lure the public into their traps for your consciousness. If you ever wonder why, after watching any of these frequency-embedded video or audio productions, you had a sense of peace, love, anxiety, fear, anger or moral outrage, you can lay your emotional reactions at the feet of Loos tampering. It's not just about what you see and hear, it is the frequency tampering that generates these emotions within you. It is not just the over-dramatic music or graphic images that spark these emotions (although those help as audio and visual reinforcement), they are only the psychological weapons used by your eyes and ears to ensure that the CNS emotional manipulations 'take' when you view this kind of psychological warfare filth.

Every one of these instances described in this chapter is deigned to either create a new narrative or belief system or play on narratives already in existence to reinforce them and ensure that people do not forsake the programming of their own specific belief narrative. It doesn't matter if it is a Christian narrative or a New Age narrative; it doesn't matter if it is a false historical conspiracy narrative or some nonsense about the Earth being flat. The only objective is to keep people roped into one herd belief system or another, so these psychological warfare tactics keep people emotionally agitated, anxious, fearful or full of a false sense of spiritual joy by embracing some spiritual escapist ideology. Control is the name of the game. They own your mind, but they can only access your mind through your emotional center first.

This is where the social network phenomenon plays into our modern electronic culture. It is because of the residual hive mind infection that we seek solace and acceptance within the group, whatever that particular group might be. As I noted previously, social networking has almost become an evil of our age because of how emotionally devastating it has become to both teens and adults. Aside from Google and Facebook secretly recording every bit of private information put on the internet, in collusion with the CIA (which started Google), we see people who have become so totally dependent on any kind of group interface with 'like-minded people' that they willingly and foolishly air all their personal laundry out there for all the world to see.

Included in these social networks, there are hundreds of other social networks available for electronic social interaction like online Bible study groups, spiritual websites, gaming websites, neo-Nazi websites and a plethora of others who all manage to function with the groupthink 'ingroup versus outgroup' mentality. Each of these types of websites have their site gurus who pick and choose who is allowed to remain so long as they conform to the groupthink of the website, and who can and are ostracized or banned by not toeing the groupthink line. I have personally witnessed so much emotional and psychological abuse on these websites that it is sickening. It is just another form of cyber-bullying and hive-indoctrinated herd discipline.

Add to all this activity your garden variety trolls that cruise news comment sections as well as YouTube comment threads and other websites who just get their kicks out of emotionally riling people up, and we have a global psychological epidemic of monumental proportions. Many of these trolls are agents provocateurs placed in these threads to intentionally keep the public's emotions in constant turmoil. They are paid agents working for the triumvirate with the specific assignment to antagonize the public and bait them into hostile online emotional conflicts. The Zionists have schools in Israel to train many of these agents, usually college students, called the Hasbara, to protect Israel's Zionist agenda and shout down any voice of dissent that challenges Israel's actions. For those who doubt this assertion I point you to the article below for verification.

https://972mag.com/hasbara-why-does-the-world-fail-to-understand-us/27551/

The psychological and emotional abuse is rampant all across the internet, and there is no one in their right mind that can deny this sordid and ugly truth. It is a mass psychosis that the field of psychology is totally inept in knowing how to cure or stop. The best the field has to offer as a solution is prescribing mind-numbing drugs or anti-depressants to people who are so emotionally handicapped that they just can't function living in this world. Doping a goodly percentage of the population is not a solution, but it does keep the profit margins of the pharmaceutical makers very high. It is this escalating outbreak of emotionally handicapped people who have been continually taught to 'get in touch with their feelings' since the Theosophy-oriented sex, drugs and rock & roll era of the 1960s that launched the Esalen Institute and the modern spiritual movement that has led our species to this impasse, all orchestrated by the industry of Psychology to begin with. Psychologists have created a disease they can't cure. This is why we see an escalating number of mental disorders filling the pages of the Diagnostic and Statistical Manual of Mental Disorders (DSM-5) on a yearly basis.

With leftist indoctrination, coupled with such a hate-filled electronic environment, with fires fueled by the Mockingbird media establishment and the elite political class pushing narratives of hate, racism, anti-Semitism and all the other emotional fodder people are subjected to day in and day out, is it any wonder we look around and think the world is going crazy? Here's a little secret --- it is! And it has not gone crazy without a tremendous influence from the field of Psychology itself. It is an artificially induced insanity, and the psychologists themselves are as insane as those they try to treat, infected with the same symptoms of the hapiym mind virus as everyone else, and so professionally arrogant that they won't even consider such a possibility as reality – let alone remotely accept responsibility for the damage the profession has done to human consciousness.

We live in a world where everyone can find something to be offended over, especially when we have a steady diet of propaganda to create outrage in one person or another over differences in political and religious ideologies. Our collective human environment is a cesspool, energetically speaking, and the waters of offense are continually churned by those we once believed were our trusted authorities. So long as anyone is looking to be offended, they will find something that offends them. So long as anyone has a herd turf to protect based on the belief in one narrative or another, they are clay in the hands of emotional manipulators who know how to control your consciousness. I will address this on the personal level in the next chapter.

14. We Are All Abusers

We are now going to get to the most difficult part of this presentation, and that is where the reader is going to have to be honest with themselves and look in the mirror and admit the truth, not avoid or deny it because it makes one uncomfortable. Everything that precedes this chapter is problem identification. This chapter is going to provide at least the foundational steps with which humanity can start to heal its consciousness from untold generations of hapiym virus infection habits and external control by those who only want to keep humanity as brainless herds of cattle to direct as they choose. This is how we all learn to take the first steps into curing the artificially and deliberately induced emotional psychosis that is the world in which we live.

The path to freedom of consciousness is fraught with psychological and emotional discomfort. This is the primary reason so few people embark on this journey to free their consciousness from the constraints imposed on us by outside forces, whether that be from instilled hapiym virus habits, or from the psychological and emotional manipulators in the world around us. As long as you are bound by any of these factors, whether it is through reactive emotions or psychological herd manipulation, you are never going to be truly free. Your consciousness and your life will simply remain a slave to the designs of others. You will never know true freedom regardless of how you lie to yourself and make yourself believe you are free.

The fact of the matter is that we all live our lives in a world of menu choices. We do not write the menu, we do not cook or create the dishes on the menus (realities), we just select our options, (what we mistakenly think is free choice), from a list of menu items called beliefs that have been created by others for us to choose from. We may shift our belief from one narrative belief system to another, but that only amounts to picking a different item from the pre-designed choices on the menu devised by others to keep us under their control. How many of you have ever viewed life in this factual context? This is how herds are created and controlled. Granted, someone may create a new menu item from time to time and create another herd ideology, but the general public remains quite content to pick from the available menu items without a lot of thought or protest. It is less cognitively challenging. This is what we refer to in our works as the first cognition. We all start this journey from the standpoint of controlled first cognition awareness. It is all any of us have been allowed to know all our lives. With the exception of a literal handful of people, humanity has never known there is another choice that leads one to a higher level of cognitive awareness that we call the second cognition. I explained the foundational principles for this in my book *Willful Evolution.*

In the field of consciousness studies, we have two points of demarcation, one is called cognitive resonance, and the other is called cognitive dissonance, based on a theory proposed by the psychologist Leon Festinger in 1957. As a general rule, most people seek to work within the framework of cognitive resonance. What this means is that all our beliefs theoretically align together to bring us a sense that all is right with our personal worldview. Confirmation bias serves as a tool to reinforce cognitive resonance. It is the easy path for the herd-indoctrinated individual to follow.

Cognitive dissonance, on the other hand, occurs when we are confronted with information or facts that disrupt our worldview (such as the facts presented in this book) and we have a choice of either acknowledging these facts, or denying them and running back into our world where our narrative of beliefs is sustained. Cognitive dissonance can occur from many different circumstances. Say your pet got run over and you just can't accept the fact that it is dead. This denial of the truth can cause that cognitive dissonance. Failure to admit that the pet is gone is an untruth, but denying this fact is only escapism even if it brings only temporary cognitive resonance. It is a simple example, but I think you get my point.

All of our beliefs are categorized and harmonized in our minds and become part of our personal identity, or at least the identity of the faux ego created by the hapiym virus. These beliefs become our psychological 'home' of cognitive resonance. Anything that supports these beliefs is fine so long as it doesn't serve to disrupt our psychological equilibrium too much. Cognitive dissonance disrupts this equilibrium and makes us want to seek whatever is necessary to get back to that point of psychological cognitive resonance. The hard fact is that no one is going to be able to free their consciousness from all the external forces that have created their illusionary reality of cognitive resonance without suffering bouts of cognitive dissonance. These can either come with great realizations of truth that pull the rug from beneath the feet of our reality, or they can be handled in smaller bouts where we slowly come to the truth about things. Whether big or small, cognitive dissonance is a *requirement* of freeing your consciousness, and the fact is that 99.9% of the public will do anything to avoid cognitive dissonance. Everyone wants their illusionary narrative world wrapped in a pretty package and they have no desire to have this narrative turned on its head or altered. It is easier to live the lie than to face the truth, and sadly, we live in a world of perceptual narrative lies.

I explained previously about how we are all sort of schizophrenic, having our basic personality, and also having this false overlaid faux personality left behind by the hapiym virus – the false ego. Everyone has this voice in their head, and when I say voice, I don't mean that we have something outside ourselves talking to us in an audio fashion. What I mean by this is that we all talk to ourselves in our minds. It is a constant train of thinking about what we are doing, or what we are going to do, and what will happen after that, and then we start playing guessing games with this inner talk, what don Juan referred to as the inner dialogue, conjuring up all sorts of 'what if' situations associated with what we think we want to do and what might mess up our plans, etc.

This inner dialogue is the voice of the residual hapiym virus' false ego talking to itself. This is the voice of doubt, anger, fear, jealousy, victimhood and every other thought and emotion you can have. There are few people out of the 7 billion inhabitants on this planet that have ever had more than a moment's silence in their own heads the length of their entire lives because of this virus habit of continually thinking and talking to ourselves in this manner. Through this inner dialogue the virus was able to stir our emotional center by continually dreaming up presumed slights by other people, playing 'what if' games continually in our minds, being offended, having our feelings hurt, pondering revenge, feeding depression or a building sense of anger. This is where the mind and emotional center of the bodymind were manipulated by the virus as a closed loop circuit in our bodies, and it was all designed to keep us emotionally reactive so the hapiym mind parasite could deplete our energies and feed itself. The virus became an invasive squatter in everyone's cognitive house.

Although the virus itself is no longer present in our species, we all carry the residual thinking and emotional habits of the virus programmed into us. Psychologists think this is the human 'norm', emotionally speaking. They have simply accepted what they have observed and not once delved into the why of emotions, as I stated earlier. As such, they have completely overlooked the idea that there may be a way to override these virus symptoms and free our consciousness and our emotions from the emotional roller coaster symptomatology of the hapiym disease. The work we have written gives instructions on exactly how one can achieve this for themselves over time, provided they have the will and the stamina to cure themselves of these virus symptoms.

Just as people wrapped up in herd narratives embrace the beliefs of the narrative and become defenders of their respected faiths and ideologies, the virus makes each of us equally defensive on a personal level when we feel the need to defend our actions with others. Although we are individuals, we all carry the herd programming into our personal lives. We do not say I *believe* in Marxism or Christianity or Islam, we say I *am* a Marxist, Christian or Muslim. In using this example, it should not be hard to understand how we fold our beliefs into our false virus personality, and then the belief becomes part of our self-identification, or that of the faux hapiym hive cell personality false ego. Under the symptoms of the virus, we *become* our beliefs. I *am* a Raiders fan or a Cowboys fan. I *am* a victim of a cruel world or a cruel society and on and on our list of identity factors build in our minds. Each of our individual beliefs, if we embrace them strongly enough, all require our defending them, for to not defend the belief, we would not be defending ourselves. Or to say it more accurately, we would not be defending the false ego identity created by the virus in your mind.

Everyone defends their actions, from the abuser to the abused, and we all feed off the energies of others. We have no choice because this is how the virus programmed us to act. We do not so much feed energetically off each other as the virus did, but we do feed psychologically on each other which does spark certain emotional gratification when we feel we come out on top of any argument or debate. We know of no other way to exist because our minds and emotions have been controlled by the symptoms of the virus our entire lives.

Each of us is a walking bag of labels. We are each a catalogue of descriptions and every description is founded on a belief of who we *think* we are without ever discovering who we really are beneath all this virus programming. Everyone has something to defend, but in the real world, there is nothing to defend beyond your personal bodily existence for survival. Everything you believe requires defending is but a cognitive illusion, a description from someone else's narrative that we happen to agree with and adopt as part of our personal identity, no different than an actor playing a role on a stage play. The genius of the hapiym mind virus is that the infection tricked us all into believing this faux ego personality, built upon nothing more than beliefs, labels and descriptions was *us*. As don Juan said, the predator *gave us their mind,* and in doing so, we also gave our mind to it and we let it trick us into giving up our personal cognitive sovereignty and freedom to a mimic virus conman who took residence in our mind.

Emotional triggers are plugged into our cell system. Since our body is made up of over 37 trillion cells, that is a lot of storage space for the hive virus infection to embed remembered triggers into our cellular memory. Any bad experience we have that has sparked a negative emotion in us was catalogued and stored in our body's cellular memory. Any time we encounter a situation that resembles the primary negative trauma that sparked the first emotional response, this cellular memory rises up and we react with the same emotion as the original trauma induced in us. Every time we experience anything that resembles this first trauma, we react emotionally the same way, time after time. Because of these negative emotional experiences, it just adds another layer on top of the original program when we experience similar situations that call up these old emotions. We are all caught in a loop of repeating emotional experiences. The field of psychology has no concept on how to cure these responses because they figure that it is normal for us to react that way. All psychologists can offer, at best, is a band-aid approach in an attempt to heal their clients. Most of the time they simply resort to prescribing anti-depressants or other drugs for people who have literally made themselves emotionally 'trigger happy' like you observe with the modern leftists. These people have psychologically programmed themselves to be victims and are constantly looking for something that offends them so they can complain about being triggered as victims – like encountering someone wearing a MAGA hat, for instance. Sadly, it is the field of psychology itself which is directly responsible for creating such faulty programming in the modern left.

Based on the virus infection and its residual habits in all of us, we each seek emotional gratification in the things we do. There is nothing wrong with being gratified over some of our actions and accomplishments as human beings, but through the virus habits, emotional gratification is a 'reward', not dissimilar from rats getting a piece of cheese if they run a maze correctly. In the case of human psychology, the emotional gratification equals the cheese, and this emotional stimulation is a direct result of the virus infection. When you can grasp this principle, then you must acknowledge that all of humanity has become emotional addicts.

Whatever belief we accept about ourselves becomes our emotional motivator and gratifier. If one has convinced themselves that they are no good and that everyone is seeking to victimize them, then they will be the victim in virtually any situation they choose because they have convinced themselves that this is true. Their emotional reward is the validation of their belief in being a victim, leading to more negative emotions, but these emotions can be equally gratifying to a victim when their false ego's self-identity is confirmed by their own self-generated emotional responses.

Most people do not see victims as abusers, but anyone who has ever known this type of perpetual victim knows that they can be some of the most supreme manipulators of the emotions of others, more so than the overbearing, arrogant asshole of a boss. Victims can suck the energy right off their target audience as they seek to take center stage as the most victimized person in the room. By playing the victim in this manner, the victim becomes the victimizer, or the abuser, all while they whine and cry about being abused and victimized. The constant demand for pity from others is literally draining on the people around them, and the wise individual who can do so, quickly makes distance between themselves and this kind of emotional abuser.

When we are in a long-lasting relationship like marriage, just to prove what I wrote above about emotional programs being embedded in our cellular memory, how many times in a marital argument, regardless of the current point of dissension, does an old gripe from years ago get brought up to manipulate your partner in the current argument? It is the fact that whatever the old incident was, the emotional hurt was never resolved, and this argument just adds another layer onto the original cellular emotional memory. By dragging up these old emotional wounds and airing them, we are seeking superiority in the war of wills in any given argument. It is just another form of emotional manipulation in order to get our own emotional gratification if we win the argument. Again, we are *all* emotional abusers in this fashion.

Our children learn to mimic the habits they observe from their parents, who are all victims of the hapiym virus infection and its emotional and psychological manipulation, so even though the virus is no longer present within our bodies, we still carry its programming to pass on to another generation, if we all don't learn to break these habits and seek to discover what it really means to be human without the programmed virus residuals controlling our psyche, our emotions and our world. We have to be the first generation to seriously take on this challenge. We have to find the courage enough to be willing to make these changes on a personal basis and we must develop the stamina to stay with the process no matter how difficult it gets when it comes to facing our own programmed psychological and emotional demons. You are much stronger than you believe you are, and it is only hollow fear that keeps anyone from facing and correcting their own virus-instilled shortcomings. The hapiym virus used fear as one of its greatest weapons to control our consciousness and keep itself the master of our lives. Humanity can no longer continue to live in a world of 'go along to get along' by continually buying someone else's narratives, particularly if those narratives beget belief systems that only serve to control our consciousness, or if those narratives mandate that we are lesser beings, that we are born in sin that can never be washed away unless the escape clause in the belief narrative says it's way is the only way, or if these narratives leave us all as second class beings based on some intellectual's assessment that we are merely cattle.

All of our work provides the tools to help people remove themselves from the quagmire of formulated narratives, including instructions on how you can do it for yourself. To free your consciousness, you are going to have to face things that your present perception of reality may call balderdash, but when you encounter new ideas, as contained in this book, you must ask yourself who wrote the narrative that makes you believe anything is balderdash? Who is your authority? Better yet, who made *them* the authority to dictate *your* reality?

The reader must understand that I am not attacking them personally, I am focusing on what controls our psyche and our emotions in as broad brush a fashion as possible, and they are merely beliefs. Nothing more than ideas. Beliefs have no feelings of their own. They do not live and breathe; they are only *ideas* and nothing more. To challenge a belief is only to challenge an idea. Are you merely a collection of ideas that shape who you think you are? I ask you to ponder this question very seriously. Why do any of us believe anything we believe? How much was plugged into us by our parents before we were old enough to think for ourselves? As children, were we given any choice other than believing what our parents said we should believe? And did they not shape many of their beliefs from the very same reason of childhood indoctrination? This is how we pass on errors of programming from generation to generation. We take what we are told, from our parents, from our teachers in school, from our political authorities, and lastly, because some dead guy hundreds of years ago told others it was so, and they believed his narrative.

Humanity lives chained to the past. We cannot move forward as a species so long as our consciousness is tied down to ancient traditions and narratives written by others. We can no longer settle for being herd animals subject to the symptoms of a dead mind virus which has controlled our species since we were created. We can no longer live as slaves to those who have appointed themselves our masters without vote, concession or our consent, and who only consider humanity to be unwashed, stupid herd animals. It's time for humanity to write its own new narrative, to discover who we really are as a species and what we can become. This will never happen so long as we wear the chains of an unchangeable past like a slave collar around our necks. The errors of the past are there to learn from, not to perpetually wallow in through living lives of repeating history and failed narrative experiments. Humanity will have no real future so long as it stays chained to the past in this manner. We must become a wiser species than this.

The global controllers can only control you through emotional manipulation. So long as they can trigger you emotionally, they own you, and you therefore do not have control over your own emotions. You are simply a malleable commodity to these tyrants. Until you can transcend such emotional and psychological manipulation and genuinely free your consciousness, you are only a slave to the whims of these self-appointed elite who know how to play your emotions like a fiddle. Sadly, most people are unwilling to believe anything this book reveals, although virtually everything within these pages can be verified with some diligent research. The question every reader must face, whether they disagree with this information or not, is whether they want to continue to live their lives as emotionally manipulated tools to agendas on a menu that they had no say in composing or not. It takes little observation to see how all mainstream media, and much of the alternative media, strive to evoke emotional responses in their viewers and listeners. If I am incorrect in this presentation, then you must ask yourself why this is so? Why are they trying so hard to evoke emotional responses in you to drive their own selective narratives, unless of course I am right, and the world as you perceive it is not what you thought it was? Ponder this deeply before you discount the information in this book out of hand. The evidence is there, you only have to see it and acknowledge it. It is at minimum a good starting point on the road to recovery from the symptoms of the hapiym mind virus.

15. Humanity Must Write its Own Narrative

With this chapter I am going to take the reader down what they think might be the deepest rabbit hole they ever encountered. I count myself a skeptic and a self-educated researcher of high caliber. I don't make this claim to put myself on a pedestal. One can't unravel some of the mysteries of humanity's past and present without possessing a skeptic's critical eye.

Every human being possesses a certain amount of gullibility once they embrace a narrative idea. Unfortunately, many do not progress much out of this gullibility factor and will buy just about as many pigs in a poke as others are willing to sell them. In my early days I had some of this gullibility, but I have always been a critical thinker and had a personal habit of back-checking what I researched through secondary and tertiary sources before I fully accepted anything. Genuine facts go a long way in removing the gullibility factor so long as they are real facts and not just more concocted nonsense to feed the senses and emotional gratification of others.

Conspiracy theories have been around for centuries and they have a narrative market all their own. Most people latch onto one aspect of a conspiracy idea and think they have everything figured out, and therefore wind up playing the game of confirmation bias to reinforce their accepted conspiracy narrative.

Because of the gullibility factor, many people who step into the conspiracy arena see a conspiracy behind every corner. When you have organizations like those associated with the Fabian-Theosophy-SPR triumvirate paying people to come up with more conspiracy nonsense to feed the gullible and muddy the waters to misdirect people away from conspiracy fact, it is not that hard to discredit those who know about the real conspiracy by interviewing the gullible and uninformed who can't string a cohesive series of thoughts together to sound remotely credible. They sound crazy, and so the media whitewashes all conspiracy ideas by using the run of the mill uninformed conspiracy wack job as the representation of all conspiracy researchers.

One of the primary research groups into conspiracy fact was the John Birch Society, formed in 1958. The Birchers are primarily pro-Christian, pro-Constitution and very anti-Communist. They are excellent historical researchers and have tracked the so-called Deep State, or Illuminati as it is more popularly known, down through the ages, offering verifiable sources to back up their claims. It's hard to argue against solid historical research. It is a result of this excellent research, and the fact that the John Birch organization is about educating the public about the real facts of U.S. history versus the sanitized version taught in our schools, that the Fabian Marxists had to discredit them. To this day the Deep State is still working to discredit the work the Birchers have done.

I have been aware of the John Birch society for a long time, but until very recently, I did not look into what they were actually teaching the public. I knew they were pro-Christian and anti-

Communist, but little else. Looking into the research videos they provide on their channel on YouTube, I only found historical information that backed up and supported my own information research, but which often went into more detail than my own work. I don't put them in the huckster column for sowing conspiracy disinformation, unlike others mentioned previously.

Because the Birchers were starting to make headway against the Fabian Marxists seeking to control and destroy the U.S. government and its people, they naturally became a targeted enemy in an information war between those who wanted to truthfully inform the public about the communist subversion in America, and the Fabian communists working to destroy America. The Birch Society has not escaped criticism for going on to 60 years now. The Fabians have done and are doing everything in their power to destroy their work to inform the American public of historical truth. Even the fake Republican party considered them far right extremists and a fringe movement because they didn't follow the mainstream Fabian narrative.

I bring up the Birchers because they stand as one of the primary examples of how the Fabian-controlled Mockingbird press goes against anyone not already in their pocket and working for them. And this brings us to some of the individuals I mentioned earlier. Let's start with David Icke. Icke has been a centerpiece in the conspiracy arena since 1990. He claims to have had psychic interface with the 'Godhead' and is a spokesperson to bring Theosophical Society-oriented metaphysical teachings to the planet. He has published over 20 books, and I read some of them years ago. Icke is a shining example of the paid shill conspiracy theorist put into the public arena by the unholy triumvirate. His fame mostly rides on the idea he professes that we have a bunch of shapeshifting humanoid lizards controlling our planet. The Queen of England is a shapeshifting lizard, don't you know?

The books that Icke peddles are filled to the brim with conspiracy theories, some partially factual and some fabricated, but it keeps his pockets full and he still fills auditoriums worldwide with those who are still gullible enough to buy his brand of conspiracy nonsense. To show that he is an agent for the opposition, Icke was given plenty of media platforms on interview shows over the years, although much of it was to allegedly ridicule him, which only reinforced the belief in the gullible that the media was only 'out to get him'. Most of the interviews were non-confrontational. This is a form of psychological programming called reverse psychology.

Now we will take a look at Michael Tsarion, the so-called "most dangerous man on earth". Like Icke, Tsarion is a well-informed individual who is articulate and who also takes selected historical facts and concocted malarkey to put his own Theosophical spin on his work. He is a strong proponent of the idea of Atlantis and claims to have intimate knowledge of that ancient non-civilization. Like Icke, he peddles a brand of Theosophical mysticism and is a devotee of Madame Helena Blavatsky by his own admission. He did a 4-part video series on this alone.

Like Icke, Tsarion was also given a public platform on many occasions, usually appearing on the *Ancient Aliens* TV show as some kind of authority on ancient civilizations and a promoter of the ancient alien theory throughout human history. These appearances on mainstream media on the *History Channel* are supposed to lend credence to the formulated false conspiracy narrative fabricated by the Fabian-Theosophical network.

Another mainstay on the *Ancient Aliens* broadcasts, as well as some ancient civilization broadcasts on the *History Channel,* is David Wilcock. Wilcock claims to be the dead psychic, Edgar Cayce, reincarnated. He is intimately associated with A.R.E., the foundation established by Cayce. Cayce is another one of those with deep ties to Freemasonry and Theosophy. Wilcock is big on the UFO thing, and Atlantis, which found its revival in the writings of Madame Blavatsky, although there is no mention of its existence beyond one or two references in Plato's writings.

These people have all continued to push the Atlantis narrative along with the mystical teachings of Theosophy to an unwitting audience, all the while gaining their kudos as 'conspiracy experts'. The fact that these people have gotten as much exposure in mainstream media outlets is telling in itself, as will become more evident as we move ahead. Leave it to say that they are paid disinformation agents who spew out their partially informed conspiracy theories coupled with mystical swill and stories about Atlantis, shapeshifting lizards ruling the planet, and metaphysical Theosophical gobbledygook designed to discredit valid researchers into conspiracy fact like the Birch Society.

The problem with disinformation and propaganda is that it is easier to hook people into the false narrative if you feed them something valid to set the propaganda hook, like some verifiable bits of historical information to give it a sense of validity. This serves as a method to establish the *bona fides* of the disinformation reporter. This is how these people use genuine historical facts ---- up to a point, and that is where the real narrative spins off into the realm of metaphysics, Atlantis, and shapeshifting lizard UFO land. The gullible individual with little to no discernment is now trapped in the disinformation narrative. These players, along with thousands of others like them, swamp YouTube with millions of disinformation videos, either about fake Theosophical spiritual and mystical teachings, or conspiracy theories like flat earth, and this is all designed to discredit genuine conspiracy research that exposes the real communist conspiracy to undermine and destroy America. These individuals refer to the Deep State as the Cabal or whichever catchword they use for their own spin.

This is not to say that all the information they offer is out and out fraud. The elements of historical truth, however, wins them millions of devoted followers worldwide who would defend them almost to the death rather than admit they are being manipulated by skilled propagandists.

As I stated, I read a few of Icke's books, and I have listened to Wilcock, Tsarion and Mark Passio, but I didn't get stuck in their narratives. I continued my research which led me to the revelations I have shared in this chapter. This is the skeptic in me, and it has served me well over the years in freeing my own consciousness.

Since the first presentation of the work in this volume was released under another title and publicized since 2019, and subsequently banned because of the original information provided in this chapter in that first release, there is now a concerted effort, particularly in the U.S., to wipe out history and anything else that doesn't conform to the Globalist agenda for total world domination.

As I wrote in one of my latest presentations, *From Dark to Light: A Voice in the Wilderness*, humanity lives in a world of perceptual illusions. The human mind is controlled by narratives that shape our perceptions of reality. Part of the story that was told in *Emotionalism* (the original title of this work) has now become anathema to the new narrative shapers of the NWO. Through the propaganda weapon surrounding the Covid-19 scare, half of humanity is scared to go outside its door without a mask. If one were to sound the 'all clear' and remove the mask and social distancing mandates, half the world will never let go of their fear to get back to normal. After a year of this incessant fear porn constantly hyped by the controlled news media, the psychological damage has already been done. If you don't believe that humanity is controlled by stories and narratives, we only have to look at the Covid-19 scare to see the proof of how manipulable humans are by the stories they are told by their authority figures.

Whatever superiority materialist scientism and medicine may have once possessed, science has now revealed itself to be nothing more than another element of the psychological emotional programming arsenal. Academics steeped in Marxist ideology have lost any credibility the educational system had as it turns everything into an issue of 'racism'. It has gotten so ridiculous that mathematics is now considered racist. Good luck in figuring out any logic behind that! The false virtue signalling about equality is belied by the actions of those who only incite the victim classes to do their bidding for the destruction of history. The only equality being sought for humanity is equality at the lowest rung of the developmental ladder. The narrative controllers want humanity to return to its status throughout the ages, as illiterate, dumbed-down serfs. The Globalist agenda is only a return to the feudalism of old. The new narrative is being shaped before your eyes. Just as every other cultural narrative in the past was shaped by turmoil and revolution. The Antifa rioters today are not one jot different than Christian or Muslim rioters and property destroyers of the past as each of those religions sought to impose their narrative realities through force and intimidation. Modern revolutionary movements all follow the same pattern going back to pre-Biblical times.

The pattern for mind control is a tried-and-true part of human manipulation, for one only has to find people they can convince are victims, and new armies of victimized revolutionaries are used as the cannon fodder to exchange old cultural narratives for new ones. Incite the emotions of the people and you create your mobs and your revolutionaries. This cannot be refuted, although many will deny the truth of it. Repeat the new narrative lies often enough, eventually through coercion, then the new narrative supplants the old, statues are torn down, books are burned, and within a generation or two no one is any the wiser. The history that was no longer exists, and the 'history' it is replaced with never happened. Thus, the world of illusion perpetuates itself, following the guidelines put forth in the Fabian Society member George Orwell's *1984*. If humanity doesn't grow some backbone and some wisdom, we are very likely looking at our species' epitaph being written, and there will likely be nothing left to remember us except mechanical robots already being manufactured to replace us.

16. Repairing Human Consciousness

Before any problem can be resolved it must first be acknowledged that not only does a problem exist, but what the root cause of the problem is. The field of Psychology has been used as a weapon against global societies since its inception, and psychologists have done more damage to the human psyche than offering any real positive mental health benefits. Regardless of those well-meaning starry-eyed souls who gravitate to the profession believing that they can help cure humanity of its mental ills, students in the field quickly learn that the practice is rigid and ossified and laden with close-minded academics who can rarely float a new idea without being banned from the profession. Psychology is as locked in the past as is everything in the first cognition world, particularly academia. It only presents a continual cycle of wash, rinse, spin, repeat, no different than the hamster wheel of repeating history we are all locked in from generation to generation.

With the importation of Eastern Indian religions to the West, in particular in the early 20th century by the Theosophical Society, and Theosophy's patchwork cultural appropriation of all religions to devise its new Marxist oriented one world religion, the psychologists who created Esalen Institute helped promote the drug culture of the 60s and 70s. Ancient Hindus were noted for their use of hallucinogenic substances to find association and communication with their gods or spirits of the dead. The later Greek philosophers also adopted this drug use as is catalogued by their use of mind-altering substances in their religious rituals.

The concept of seeking the Divine through drug use is ancient indeed and I explained the whys of this in *Gutting Mysticism*. It did not start with the hippies in the 60s, although with the advent of what is known as Transpersonal Psychology, which also endorses such practices, it matured into the New Age religions and the occult traditions that also had a revival during the 60s and 70s. It is not my place to rehash the extensive data on all these matters that I have presented in my other books, but let it be known that none of what has happened to Western culture was by accident or happenstance. It was done by intentional sinister design of people who wanted nothing but worker drones so they could sit on their ill-gotten pinnacles of stolen wealth and power while the lowly human cattle were nothing more than their servants. The more ignorant we were, the better situated they were to rule us.

The so-called elite have waged a secret and silent war against human consciousness, and they were so perfidious that they never bothered to inform us we were under attack. Their weapon of choice was the field of psychology and the continual spinning of false narratives to ensnare our consciousness and keep us from paying attention to what they were doing to us. It has taken 5 generations of Americans for this dumbing down process to exhibit itself in full, but with the modern millennials we are staring in the face of generations lost to brainwashed mind control, not functioning with critical thinking and logic, but ruled by pure raw emotions. When emotions override the thinking process, there is no place for reason to roost in the psyche.

I have done everything in my power to explain how our emotions are governed by the nervous system and also provided substantial evidence about technology that is being used as subversive weapons to control our emotional states, and subsequently, our minds. All it takes is a glance at any news station to see how every network, and I do mean *every* network, makes their bottom-line profit margins by riling people's emotions. The preferred emotional weapons are fear, anxiety and anger in all these broadcasts. Sadly, all too many people take the bait and play the game of the hostile narrative that sets the stage of our present political environment. Where in the past it was a contest of ideas that set the political stage, now it is a contest of emotions with all rationality removed from the process. The Fabian leftists have no new ideas to present as their political platform beyond the expansion of Marxist communist policies and fear tactic narratives (global warming, save the planet, get Trump, etc.). Their entire political platform at this time is based on hate Trump and the constant propaganda to drive this emotional agenda forward from their controlled media outlets 24 hours a day 7 days a week. CNN has an exclusive contract as the only news network broadcast in every airport in America and the Communist left-wing media, being the propaganda wing of the Communist Democrat party, is only an echo chamber of the rabid Communist Democrats in Washington, D.C.

Probably 2/3 of the American public has completely stopped paying any attention to the political process anymore because they are most likely suffering from a form of emotional PTSD. The constant overload of emotional conflict and hate-laden news has driven them to the realm of seeking escapism just to try and find some level of emotional equanimity. Our population's nervous system is under constant assault, even when we believe we are just relaxing and watching television as evidenced by the very existence of the Loos patents. This constant emotional overload has led to more diagnoses of mental disorders such as people actually believing that there are over 63 gender variants beyond the biological male and female. The fact that legislation has been enacted to legitimize such mental disorders and those who are diagnosed with them as a protected minority class only further illustrates the fact that we live in a free-range insane asylum with the political inmates guarding the doors, legislatively putting the rubber stamp of approval on this type of psychosis.

One need only look to the election night returns of the 2016 election to see the emotional instability exhibited by all those supporters of Hillary Clinton when the impossible happened and Trump won the election, to see the fragility of the American psyche at this point in our history. What's wrong with this picture? Immediately after this loss on election night we saw the screaming and wailing of the Hillary supporters televised round the world, and by the next day thousands of emotionally crushed individuals took to broadcasting their emotional pain all over YouTube, crying and gnashing over nothing more than the loss of a national election. These were all exhibitions of raw emotions with no thinking processes in place by these individuals to govern their behavior. It is fully illustrative of the emotional instability present in our society as the Marxists seek to destroy this nation from within. To date, they have done a very effective job of nearing their goals.

When the Democrats won the House of Representatives majority in 2018, it was time to put the focus on the conservative right to instill the fear necessary to rule the right-wing's emotions by promoting issues like late term abortions and bravely endorsing out and out infanticide by the Democrat party. The insanity only amplified to gather in the entire country and separate it into almost warring camps. The words 'civil war' are being floated over these emotionally driven issues, and it yet remains to be seen if emotions over these issues, no different than the raw emotions garnered by the Abolitionists of the 19th century who stirred up the emotions of the public to create the first Civil War, will win again. The issues may be different, but the emotional tableau is the same and humanity hasn't learned a thing from its past. We stand on the verge of repeating history once again and there is nary a sane voice to be found in the mix on either the left or the right. Fear and anger rule the American psyche at this point, except for those who have completely checked out, reliant on alcohol, drugs, video game addiction, pursuing fruitless entertainment options or have just gone into an emotional fugue and live their lives on drugs prescribed by our esteemed psychologists. At the center of all of this lies a manipulated nervous system to jack up people's emotions. The hapiym virus may be dead, but the Loos devices have stepped in to take its place.

The processes we have devised and used on ourselves with the foundational understanding shared in this book have provided us with a cure to this malady of over-emotionalism. Through a process of cell talk to root out the most pernicious of these hidden emotional programs, coupled with a discipline to alter our thinking by accepting uncomfortable truth over comfortable lies, anyone can transcend this chaotic first cognition world and come out cognitively whole on the other side at the second cognition. Unfortunately, because everyone's life circumstances are different, there is no 'group' solution to this problem. It is a process that must be undertaken by the individual because everyone's individual cellular programming is different from the next person.

There is no cookie cutter solution that applies to all people in all places around the planet, so the process of this change will be as slow as it takes to find people who will accept the challenge to change themselves for the better. It may take generations, or it may fail altogether. Humanity stands at the greatest crossroad it has ever faced and our choice is simple, do we want freedom, or do we want a future of tyranny where 99% of humanity is ruled by a corrupt and tyrannical elite 1% of the population as we have been throughout our entire existence as a species? This is the greatest problem facing humanity amidst the plethora of issues that beleaguer our consciousness and continually assault and fatigue our emotions. Emotionalism and emotional manipulation, conjoined with the abuse of psychology as a weapon, are the root of all the evils humanity presently faces. This is reducing the problem to its base element. We can either step into the Fabian-authored world of *1984*, or another Fabian-authored *Brave New World*. Both George Orwell and Aldous Huxley were members of the Fabian Society, each of whom allegedly walked away from the organization, but their novels have left humanity with nothing but bad choices where the elite will rule, and the rest of humanity will be nothing but brainwashed terrorized slaves to some Big Brother end game for humanity, or a society of heavily drug-dependent, ignorant worker drones. This is not where humanity is headed, this is the road we are *already on* and it leads only to destruction. A third lesser-known Fabian dystopian novel was written by Ira Levin, the author of *Rosemary's Baby* entitled, *This Perfect Day*. Elements of all three of these novels are present in our world today and the outcome of this combination is pretty grim for humanity as a whole unless we choose to do something to stop it and change direction from our present narrative-dictated path.

I did not write this book to titillate or frighten the reader, regardless of the content presented. I wrote this book to advise those who are still willing to read a book to know that there is a way out of this cognitive sewer of living narratives, traditions and beliefs handed down to us by others who never had humanity's best interests at heart. In a world where most people are so cognitively handicapped and whose attention span rarely goes beyond about 10 minutes looking for soundbite explanations to complex issues, it is few people who will even take the time to read a book, even if you give it away (I can attest to the fact from firsthand knowledge). Through psychological manipulation coupled with technologies that change virtually every week, everyone is impatient. They seek instant gratification, which in itself is just another form of emotional reward. Pacify the emotions and don't bother me with thinking, it's too hard! This is the mantra of the culture in which we live – "I want what I want, and I want it now!" Our technology is advancing faster than we can keep up with while our emotions lie in a state of arrested development. We have not exhibited the intelligence to master the technologies we create and are quickly becoming slaves to them. If you disagree with this, try taking a cell phone or iPad away from your kid and see the kicking and screaming that ensues when they can no longer play in their online herds. Hell, take the cell phone away from most adults addicted to them and you will see the same emotional reactions.

Until humanity, or at least the wiser portion of humanity, realizes that what our science has presumed to be the human norm where our emotions are concerned is in fact an artificially amplified byproduct of an energetic mind virus infection, then we will remain exactly where we are as a species – on a downward spiral to mass destruction at our own hands as emotionally volatile, non-thinking individuals who can think of nothing more than self-gratification or killing their adversaries based on manipulated emotions. Fear, anger and rigidity in continually perpetuating beliefs based on someone else's narratives will lead this species to destruction, with mass wholesale killings on the horizon if we don't make the individual decision to change ourselves and transcend into something better while we have the time to do it. One only needs to look at the world around them to see this hostility escalating on an almost daily basis.

We are all sitting on a cultural powder keg of emotional violence and there are forces in this world who would love nothing better than to ignite the fuse to set off that powder keg of irrational emotions and have us kill each other in the streets. You are now apprised that there is a way out of this being continually manipulated by others. The question now is what you, personally, intend to do about it.

Afterword

Although the contents of this book are grim and hard to accept, the design of this volume is to help people free their consciousness from the chains that bind our minds through our emotions. Humanity must grow the wisdom to see through the perceptual narrative illusions that keep our minds enslaved to stories designed to keep us as nothing more than manipulable cattle to those who shape the narratives.

Humanity has a path to our species advancement that most people cannot remotely imagine. We are so locked in to so many false narratives, and each of these narratives paints an ending that the narrative composer wants us to see or believe, and we can imagine no outcome for humanity beyond what we have been told or what has been 'written' in these narratives. We are slaves to the words of others. We have lived the narratives of others for so long that we are utterly clueless about what it takes to write our own narrative, either as individuals or as a species.

Humanity has been governed and controlled by untrustworthy authorities and intellectual classes for so long that it doesn't know how to think for itself. The concept of self-rule is a great idea, but how to manage such an affair goes beyond the ken of the average person with all the obedience and reliance on authority programming that blinds them to any other viable alternative. Humanity is not presently equipped to take on such an assignment.

No one can face the millennia's long progression of this tyranny in one fell swoop. It is too massive to digest in one sitting by anyone. The shock of cognitive dissonance is too massive for the human psyche to take at this time, so elements of the conspiracy must be digested steps at a time. I realize that what is contained in this volume has probably shocked the conscious of many readers, but trust me when I tell you, it is still only part of the bigger puzzle of tyranny yet to be revealed.

As we encounter new information that disrupts our narrative worldview, we all face the difficult emotional and psychological disruption of cognitive dissonance. It can't be avoided. It comes with the territory. Each of our books strips away different layers of the lies. There are different methods for revealing the lies that expose the narrative illusions, and as reluctant as humanity is to face these lies we believe to be reality, we hold a vision for a brighter future for all humanity. This vision cannot and will not be achieved so long as the world remains enslaved to narratives not of their making; and changing it starts one person at a time. Each individual is responsible for themselves first and foremost, for the internal work of ridding themselves of the residual virus habits can only be done on an individual basis. No one can do it for you. It is solely your responsibility. Our books offer the guidelines on how those who have the courage to not only face a new tomorrow but can become participants as script writers for a wide-open future for human advancement – provided that humanity is willing to free their consciousness from the cognitive and emotional slavery exposed in this book. It's a dirty job, but someone has to do it, and we need a lot of someone's on this project.

<u>Addendum</u>

Since the original manuscript of this book was written, released, and subsequently banned the Marxist left has all but taken over America. The former Nations' Capitol is now surrounded with high steel fencing and concertina wire and guarded with military personnel. The corruption of government has been exposed through every branch laid out in the Constitution – the Legislative, Executive and Judicial. The nation is still paralyzed by the Covid virus scare as more businesses are forced to shut down and people being forced into financial destitution as a result of the draconian measures being enforced with nothing more than propaganda and innuendo to keep the new narrative thriving. Everything is racist except racists screaming about racism.

The surveillance society on the Communist Chinese model is almost totally in effect and the U.S. is quickly heading down the road to extinction as a nation state. And all this was done without firing a shot. It was accomplished through psychological manipulation over the span of about 120 years. Whether there is any threat to 5G frequency manipulation as so many decry, I can't say at this point. Yet, what I have presented about the Loos devices and psychology in this book is still in use and has had a devastating effect on cultures worldwide. Whether humanity chooses to recover from this type of warfare remains to be seen. Right now, it looks rather grim.

References

Le Bon, Gustave – *The Crowd: A Study of the Popular Mind (1895)*

Le Bon, Gustave – *The Psychology of Socialism (1898)*

Beall, Endall - *The Psychology of Becoming Human: Evolving Beyond Psychological Conditioning (2018)*

Sargant, William - *Battle for the Mind: A Physiology of Conversion and Brain -Washing (1994)*

Bernays, Edward – *Propaganda (1928)*

Hitler, Adolf – *Mein Kampf (1925)*

Ellwood, Robert S. – *Theosophy on War and Peace (article 2003)* https://www.theosophical.org/publications/1606

Beall, Endall & Mrs. Endall - *Revamping Psychology: A Critique of Transpersonal Psychology (2015)*

Beall, Endall - *Gutting Mysticism: Explaining the Roots of All Supernatural Beliefs (2018)*

Erich von Daniken – *Chariots of the Gods (1968)*

Sitchin, Zechariah – *The 12th Planet (1976)*

Temple, Robert K.G. – *The Sirius Mystery (1976)*

Beall, Endall - *The Energetic War Against Humanity: The 6,000 Year War Against Human Cognitive Advancement (2016)*

Forbes, Jack – *Columbus and Other Cannibals (1992)*

Levy, Paul - *Wetiko: The Greatest Epidemic Sickness Know to Humanity (2011 – out of print)*

- *Dispelling Wetiko: Breaking the Curse of Evil (2013)*

Wilson, Colin – *The Mind Parasites (1967)*

Jung, Carl – *The Red Book (2009)*

Beall, Endall – *We Are Not Alone – Parts 1-3 (2015-2016)*

Orwell, George – *1984 (1949)*

Huxley, Aldous – *Brave New World (1932)*

Levin, Ira – *This Perfect Day (1970)*

Beall, Endall – *Willful Evolution (2015)*

Wikipedia references:

Brainwashing

Psychological Warfare

Mockingbird

Bloody Code

Humanitarianism

Lucis Trust

Code of Hammurabi

Albigensian Crusade

Associative Memory

Operant Conditioning

Hebbian Theory

Donald O. Hebb

Spike-timing-dependent plasticity

Groupthink

The Evolution of Consciousness Series

Book 1

A Philosophy for the Average Man: An Uncommon Solution to a World Without Common Sense by Endall Beall

Book 2

Willful Evolution: The Path to Advanced Cognitive Awareness and a Personal Shift in Consciousness by Endall Beall

Book 3

Demystifying the Mystical: Exposing Myths of the Mystical and the Supernatural by Providing Solutions to the Spirit Path and Human Evolution by Endall Beall

Book 4

Navigating into the Second Cognition: The Map for your journey into higher Conscious Awareness by Endall Beall

Book 5

The Energy Experience: Energy work for the Second Cognition by Mrs. Endall Beall

Book 6

We Are Not Alone – Part 1: Advancing Cognitive Awareness in an Interactive Universe by Endall Beall

Book 7

We Are Not Alone – Part 2: Advancing Cognitive Awareness through Historical Revelations - Endall Beall

Book 8

Advanced Teachings for the Second Cognition by Mrs. Endall Beall

Book 9

We Are Not Alone – Part 3: The Luciferian Agenda of the Mother Goddess by Endall Beall

Companion Volumes to The Evolution of Consciousness Series

False Prophecies, Reassessing Buddha and the Call to the Second Cognition by Endall Beall

Operator's Manual for the True Spirit Warrior by Endall Beall

Spiritual Pragmatism: A Practical Approach to Spirit Work in a World Controlled by Ego by Endall Beall

Revamping Psychology: A Critique of Transpersonal Psychology Viewed From the Second Cognition by Endall Beall & Mrs. Endall Beall

The Common Sense Revolution: Creating Common Ground and Genuine Common Sense – Endall Beall and the Psoyca Crew (2016)

Second Cognition Series

Book 1

The New Paradigm Transcripts: Teachings for a New Tomorrow by Endall Beall & Doug Michael

Book 2

Breaking the Chains of the First Cognition: Tools for Understanding the Path to the Second Cognition by Endall Beall & Doug Michael

Book 3

PSOYCA – Road to the Second Cognition by Endall Beall & Doug Michael

Book 4

The Energetic War Against Humanity: The 6,000 Year War Against Human Cognitive Advancement by Endall Beall

Book 5

The Cognitive Illusion of History: How Humanity Has Been Controlled Through Selective and Biased Historical Reporting by Endall Beall & Doug Michael

Book 6

The Second Cognition Toolbox: Requirements for Advancing Your Consciousness by Endall Beall

Book 7

Firestarters: The Gemma and Endall Transcripts – by Endall Beall and Gemma Beall

Book 8

No Trespassing: Creating a New World Based on Mutual Respect by Endall Beall

Book 9

Psoyca Consciousness by Endall Beall

Companion Volumes to the Second Cognition Series

Understanding Wisdom: A Treatise on Wisdom Viewed from the Second Cognition by Endall Beall

From Belief to Truth – From Truth to Wisdom by Endall Beall

The Psychology of Becoming Human: Evolving Beyond Psychological Conditioning by Endall Beall

Standalone Work: Available for free .pdf download at our website

Clarifying the don Juan Teachings for the Second Cognition: A Pragmatic Reanalysis Without the Mystical Misdirection – by Endall Beall

Beyond Don Juan: Into the Third Attention – The Second Cognition (2019) - by Endall Beall

Consciousness Evolves, Intellect Doesn't: Why Humanity Can't Advance its Consciousness (2020) – by Endall Beall

Find free pdf downloads for these books at the links below, or look for them under the header of Companion Books to the Series at our website https://www.demystifyingthemystical.com/#/

https://www.demystifyingthemystical.com/#/book/17

https://www.demystifyingthemystical.com/#/book/64

https://www.demystifyingthemystical.com/#/book/65

Beyond Second Cognition Series

Book 1

Gutting Mysticism: Explaining the Roots of All Supernatural Belief by Endall Beall (2018) by Endall Beall

Book 2

Religion, the Goddess and the Mind Virus of Heaven: The Deception of Holiness in Human Belief Systems (2018) by Endall Beall

Book 3

Introduction to the Multiverse: The Layman's Guide to the Cosmos (2018) by Endall Beall

Book 4

Facing the Truth: Conspiracy or Plan? 100 Years of Subversive Psychological Warfare Against America by Endall Beall (2018)

Book 5

The No Rules Multiverse: The Endeavor to Repair a Faulty Creation by Endall Beall (2019)

Book 6

Into the Hinterlands: Beyond Second Cognition) by Endall Beall (2019

Book 7

Mission Earth: Advanced Messages for Psoyca Ground Crew – (2020) – Endall Beall

Book 8

Voodoo Reality: The Strangeness of Creation by Endall Beall (2020)

Book 9

The Flesh Robot: The Truth About the Human Computer by Endall Beall (2020)

Book 10
The Flesh Robot – Part 2: Explaining the Nature of the Cosmos and How it is Changing by Endall Beall (2020)

Companion Volumes to Beyond Second Cognition Series

Emotionalism: How the Human Herds are Controlled by Endall Beall (2019) (Banned and censored 2021)

Electronic Frequencies and Mind Control: What Science, Psychology and Academia Can't Tell the Public – Endall Beall (Edited reprint of the *Emotionalism* book above)

The Truth About the 'Divine' Soul: The Late Creation of the Concept of Heaven by Endall Beall (2019)

Challenging Philosophy and the Philosophers" Explaining Nietzsche to Philosophical Academia by Endall Beall (2019)

Explaining the Shift in Consciousness: Translating the 'Becoming' book from the New Paradigm Trilogy by Endall Beall (2020)

The End of the World as We Know It: A New World for Advanced Consciousness by Endall Beall (2020)

Facing the Truth – Redux: What the Great Awakening is About by Endall Beall (2020)

Into the Hinterlands Series

Book 1

The New Great Awakening: What People Think it Means and What it Actually Portends by Endall Beall (2020)

Book 2

End Times or a New Beginning?: Humanity's Moment to Evolve by Endall Beall (2020)

Book 3

True Enlightenment: How Humanity Has Gotten it Wrong by Endall Beall (2020)

Book 4

From Dark to Light: A Voice in the Wilderness by Endall Beall (2021)

Book 5

The Actuality: The Process of Life by Endall Beall (2021)

Companion Volumes to the Into the Hinterlands Series

The Afterlife: Religion and Spirituality's Psychological Weapon Against Humanity by Endall Beall (2020)

Upcoming Volumes

The Denial Species: Humanity's Unwillingness to Advance its Consciousness by Endall Beall

The Freedom Factor: Subjective Reality: Infinite Variations by Endall Beall

Integration: Humanity's 'Knowing' Mergence with Consciousness by Endall Beall

For questions or inquiries contact the authors at *http://demystifyingthemystical.com/#/*

Further work by these authors can be found at the Gemma Beall YouTube channel at
https://www.youtube.com/channel/UCN3VfiNrozRSUBi DIR8k9EA

Video podcasts can also be found at our Rumble page at Willful Evolution at the link below
https://rumble.com/c/c-405017

Or through the Gemma Beall Patreon website for subscriptions of $5 per month for access to over 600 video and podcast presentations, and $15 per month for all the videos and an expanding number of educational discussions, chapter previews, blogs and an interactive community forum.

https://www.patreon.com/GemmaBeall/

www.ingramcontent.com/pod-product-compliance
Lightning Source LLC
Chambersburg PA
CBHW070113260726
48658CB00001B/92